A Journey of Soles

Lands End to John O'Groats

Kathy Trimmer and Ranger

To Margaret

Thanks for sharing walks
and love of walking with us

Kathy Trimmer

HAYLOFT

Ranger & Ken

First published 2003

Hayloft Publishing Ltd., Kirkby Stephen,
Cumbria, CA17 4EU.

tel: (017683) 42300
fax. (017683) 41568
e-mail: dawn@hayloft.org.uk
web: www.hayloft.org.uk

ISBN 1 904524 05 2

A catalogue record for this book is available
from the British Library

Cover photograph by Peter Koronka
Maps by Ken Trimmer
Cartoons by 'Smoutie'

Produced in Great Britain
Printed and bound in Hungary

for Ken, my sole mate

.

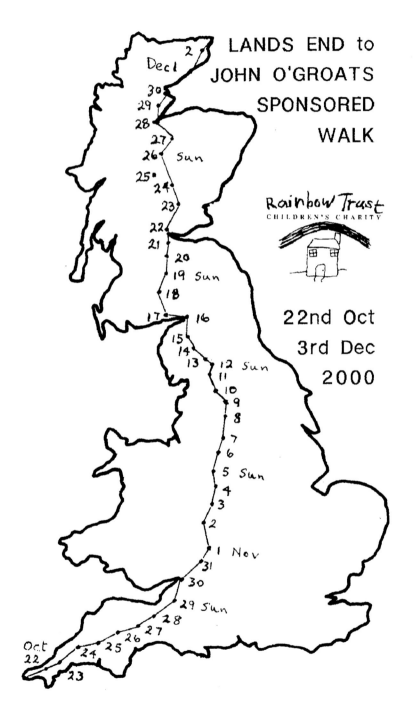

CONTENTS

THE BEGINNING BY RANGER
21 October, 2000, 8.30am

One hour behind schedule already. How can we be late leaving on an adventure that has been four years in planning and a whole year in fine-tuning? The 'team' consists of me, Ranger, star of the show, Labrador bitch, (but not at all bitchy) aged two and half; Peter who will drive our mini bus which my owner Ken has converted to a camper van and the said Ken and Kathy, idiots who decided to take me to walk the length of Great Britain, a distance of almost a thousand miles.

The idea was conceived before I was, when they had been involved in guiding two men called Ivan and Alan, one blind and one partially sighted,

who walked from Lands End to John O'Groats in 1996 for charity. They were appealing to people to help guide them through the area where we live. Ivan and Alan took sixty days to do the walk. We're planning to do it in 43 days at an average of 22 miles per day. Another blind chap we know, George Jones from Shropshire, did it in an amazing time of 31 days at the age of 65. He has a bit of tunnel vision and walked unaccompanied with a back-up vehicle.

If you believe that the 21st century doesn't really begin until 1 January, 2001, as many people do, we will have the honour, assuming we finish of course, of being the last people to complete the walk in the 20th century. The last walkers this year, apart from us, are already well on the way and due to finish at Lands End in mid November.

We follow in the footsteps of many people, all with something in common, and that is a sense of adventure combined with some degree of eccentricity. The first person to do the walk and attract a great deal of media interest was Dr. Barbara Moore in 1962. She did it with no support and lived mainly on fruit juice and raw vegetables.

The other name that is associated with the walk is Ian Botham. He has walked it twice, in 1985 and in 1999. He had lots of support, including

Photograph courtesy of the Cornwall and IOS press.

his physiotherapist who followed him all the way by car and took him to a comfortable hotel for a massage and no doubt a meal that consisted of something more exciting than raw vegetables each night. He would be the first to heap praise on people doing what we're doing, cadging beds and sleeping in a camper van, when we have it available, and walking without any back up for about 500 miles, but we have a great deal of admiration for anyone who has done it once. To do it a second time you must need to be completely potty!

Most people tackle the walk southbound for some obscure reason. I wonder why? You're far more likely to have the wind on your back walking northbound. Someone suggested it's all uphill going north because you're going up the page on the map all the time. I think the reason is that most of the population of Great Britain live closer to Lands End than John O'Groats and they feel that they are walking towards home and the possibility of a big finish with friends greeting them on their arrival. Maybe it's just the name. Why Lands End? It's certainly not Lands End as far as we're concerned, it's Lands Beginning!

Ken insists that it's Lands End because, while working in Cambourne many years ago, he became an honourary member of the Lands End Committee whose duties include standing on Lands End on windy days to make sure that it doesn't curl up. If you fail to attend when called to duty, you have to buy a beer for the rest of the committee. I did warn you that I was walking with a pair of idiots!

When talking about the walk to friends, people had asked us if we were being sponsored. A neighbour, Mollie Young, is a volunteer fund raiser for Rainbow Trust Children's Charity. They provide support for families unfortunate enough to have a very sick or terminally ill child. The support they provide is for the whole family, taking care of brothers and sisters and helping parents cope in an often devastating situation. They have two centres where families can take a break together, taking pressure off the parents for a few days while someone else does the cooking and helping the children have as much fun as possible.

Mollie offered to be our 'anchor man' back at base so Mollie is the fifth member of the team. She, together with the staff at Rainbow Trust have handled our publicity, helped us get permission to do street collections along the route and provided us with T-shirts and a collecting bucket which we intend carrying the whole way with us. Not expensive items but Rainbow Trust don't have a lot of money and they certainly don't waste any.

The reason we're already behind schedule could have something to do with what happened last night. Our neighbours decided to throw a leaving party for us. For heaven's sake, we'll be back at home in three weeks! Our home happens be almost exactly half way between Lands End and John O'Groats. Perhaps they're hoping we'll get lost, which we probably will. If you saw where we lived, you would ask 'what neighbours?' You can only see one other house from ours. Anyway there were about forty people, only three of which had travelled more than a mile to be there. About half were kids, mostly from the local primary school which we will pass in three weeks time.

Ken and Kathy (that takes up too much space, hence forth I will refer to them as the 2Ks) went into school assembly last week and took a map of Great Britain with the route marked on and told all the children about our walk and they promised to say a prayer for us when we leave. Believe me, we'll need it! They are going to walk with us for a couple of miles when we pass their school in three weeks time.

The 2Ks also went to the school in the next village, Orton, and left a map with them and they will hopefully walk from their school to meet us on the same day. Apparently they based the whole of school assembly the following day on our map... maths, geography, history, geology, sociology and several other 'ologies'. They're all there somewhere between Lands End and John O'Groats.

The children were given the opportunity to ask questions and one little chap asked how long we intended staying at John O'Groats. He couldn't quite understand that we were going to take seven weeks to get there and didn't really have any plans to stay there!

Mollie has been in touch with our MP and he's threatening to walk with us for a mile or so as well. The other thing that delayed our packing yesterday was yet another television feature, this time for *Northwest Tonight* which is a bigger deal than the last one we did for Border Television a few weeks ago.

Anyway, much like the last one, I was paraded up and down the road in the rain (why do television cameras always bring rain with them?) and up the field. Then they did some filming inside and I got to sit at the dining table with 'the team' and was filmed with my paw on the map. Mollie and Ken also had their paws on the map and when we saw it later that evening on the telly, my paw looked like, well, my paw, Mollie's fingers looked beautiful with her red painted nails but Ken's fingers were a disgrace. He might have washed his hands!

Anyway, this television interview had a bonus because I was then taken into town (Kirkby Stephen really is a town, even though everyone thinks it's a village). I was filmed being taken to the butcher's shop and given a bone to take on my walk. The 2Ks went to the greengrocer's shop to collect a lovely box of fruit that had been donated.

Actually, I don't care too much for fruit but my provisions for most of the route have already been taken care of. Because the camper van won't be with us all the time, the 2Ks will have to carry all their clobber in their rucksacks for about half of the journey and have left parcels of my dried food at strategic points along the route with people they have cadged beds with. I'm not a fussy eater, I'll eat anything and everything but they're fussy about my food and don't want me to get 'holiday tummy'.

The shop in between the butcher's and the greengrocer's is Pete Denby's, Gentleman's Outfitters and 'gear shop'. Pete also sells quite a lot of ex-army stuff and will always give you a full history of anything before he sells it to you. Ken refers to it as 'Auntie Wainwrights' (from the television programme *Last of the Summer Wine*), because you never come out of there without something in you hand, even if it's only last year's Settle-Carlisle Railway Timetable.

The start with Derek and Sheila.

About ten years ago there were two momentous events in Kirkby Stephen: It had it's first ever official Royal visit when The Queen came to do the things that queens do, open something. It seems they never close things don't queens. I'm not sure of the date but I do know what time she arrived - she arrived at Kirkby Stephen West Railway Station at precisely 10.00am. The reason everyone knows the time she arrived was that the station clock, which hadn't worked for years, was set at ten o'clock and thus has remained ever since.

Anyway, the other momentous event was that, in honour of the Royal visitor, Pete Denby cleaned his shop windows. Pete really is one of life's characters. Not as young and fit as he was, but he has been a great walk-er in his time and helped to found Kirkby Stephen Fell Rescue Team. Many people walking the Coast to Coast footpath call into Pete's shop. He's planning on retiring in the next couple of years to spend more time travelling the British Isles in his camper van and Kirkby Stephen will be a sadder place without him. He persuaded one of his suppliers to give the 2Ks some really good boots and another one to give them some 1000 mile blister free socks. (Actually, I've never seen a sock with blisters!)

The fund raising has given an extra dimension to the walk and Mollie is doing an excellent job with publicity. We've sent sponsorship forms to everyone we know and, as a result, we've been offered beds for most nights of our walk so won't need to spend too many nights in the camper van. Not that it's too bad; their bed has a spring interior mattress and a down duvet. I have an old candlewick bedspread. We have a cooker, a sink and a plug in Esky, an insulated picnic box to those who have never been to Australia. Australians don't waste words and the name is short-ened from the word Eskimo - something cold.

However, tonight we are sleeping in a bed at Mevagissey where the 2Ks have a friend, a sprightly 75-year-old called Derek Hopkins. It's been so embarrassing to be within earshot of that pair for the last six months. "Where are you staying?" people would enquire. "Where do you live?" They would reply.

Despite the fact that the route was planned to take in as many free nights B&B as possible, it is fairly straight. We will walk through Cornwall and Devon on minor roads and footpaths and then pick up the Gloucester & Sharpness Canal. We will follow the River Severn, Staffordshire & Worcester Canal, Trent and Mersey Canal and the Huddersfield High Peak Canals.

That will take us to Manchester and then we'll follow the Rochdale Canal and join the Pennine Way, loosely following it to Lothersdale and then diverting via Settle and Dent to home. By then we will be half way through the walk. The second half will again be on minor roads and footpaths until we join the new cycle path, which follows the A9 and takes us almost all the way to John O'Groats, or Lands End to us. We had toyed with the idea of a more heroic route to take in Offa's Dike, the West Highland Way, Rannoch Moor and a few General Wade military roads, but walking at this time of year, the weather might throw a few interesting things at us.

It's not really a very sensible time of year to set out but they don't do sensible, not the 2Ks. Apart from that, we do have to work for a living, all of us. I guide walkers across the fell round where we live so this really is a bus man's holiday. Those two come as well but they'd never find the way home again without me.

Walking on canal tow paths must be the easiest way of walking. It's flat, until you come to a lock of course. It's mostly quite easy on your feet, or paws in my case and I can be off my lead. I'm also quite a good swimmer so I might swim part of the way although I don't think I'll tell my sponsors or they might not cough up.

We've already had over £5,000 of sponsorship money, mostly for me, not the 2Ks. We had one cheque for £20.20 - twenty pounds for me and ten pence each for those two. Our fund raising was given a kick start by a friend of the 2Ks, Hugh Symonds who did a slide presentation for us about a run he did ten years ago when he ran all the 3000 foot plus mountains of Britain, 296 in all, running every step in between. He then ran to the ferry to Ireland and ran all the 3000 footers there as well. The total journey was over 2000 miles, more than twice as much as ours, and we're not doing mountains. Makes our walk sound like a Sunday afternoon stroll!

What was just as amazing was the fact that his backup team consisted of his wife Pauline and their three children, aged four, six and eight. They followed him on his epic three-month-long journey in a camper van. We called to see Hugh at his home near Sedbergh just before he did the slide show. There was no one in but we saw three people running towards the house. The first two, long lean lads, ran past us, looking like they had just jogged to the end of the drive. The last one was Hugh. He was wet through with perspiration. I have never seen anyone that wasn't in a swimming pool with that much liquid attached to them. Hugh and Pauline must be so proud of all their children. Their adventure raised £25,000 for Intermediate Technology. They wrote a book about their adventure and it was Hugh who told Kathy she could write a book about ours. She doesn't think she can, so I have to do it for her. Such is life!

When we arrived at Mevagissey we suddenly realised we had a big problem. It is stunning. We wanted to stay for a week. It has a lovely harbour and was famous for pilchard fishing until pilchards became scarce in the 19th century. Then it became a great place for smuggling. We wriggled the camper van through the tiny narrow streets and, of course, as women do, Kathy demanded that we stop outside a shop so that she could nip in and buy some clotted cream to go with the blackcurrant crumble she had brought as our contribution to the evening meal.

Derek has the most beautiful bungalow, up on the hill overlooking the harbour. You need a map and compass to find your way round it. I shared a boudoir with the 2Ks and lucky Peter had a room to himself. A meal was produced, maps were pawed over then it was off to bed. We needed to be up early tomorrow for the one and a half hour drive to Lands Beginning and the beginning of our adventure.

WE'RE OFF

Sunday, 22 October, Day One, 24 Miles

Lands End to Cambourne, on minor roads, footpaths and one mile on the A30

Derek has been fairly recently widowed and has regularly been going out walking with a lady called Sheila who makes lovely jam, and joined us for breakfast. She very generously gave us a nice little book about Cornwall. We set off at 7.30am, before it was fully light, leaving Derek and Sheila with the washing up. They followed on later to meet us at Lands Beginning to cross the start line and walk a mile or two with us. Our destination tonight is Cambourne, where we will sleep in the camper van and Peter will sleep in his tent. Tomorrow we finish at Indian Queens, which is about 20 miles from Mevagissey and Derek has invited us back to his place for the night.

As the day dawns, we drive away into a very beautiful landscape: ribbons of low mist and large expanses of sea. We don't often see the sea so these lovely views are a real treat. It looked like the weather was going to be kind to us on our first morning. At Lands Beginning we are

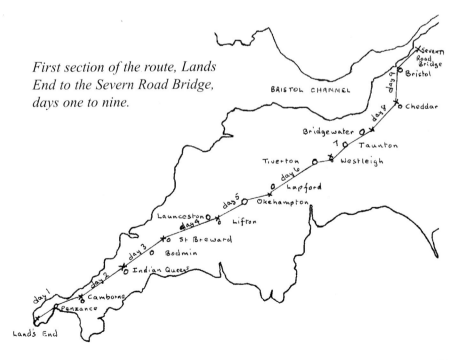

First section of the route, Lands End to the Severn Road Bridge, days one to nine.

met by a photographer from the *Western Morning News* and photographed for tomorrow's edition. They'd better put us on the front page
or else...

We went to register our departure at the hotel and then wrote postcards
to the Rainbow Trust, our two local schools and our neighbours who'd
given us such a wonderful send off. Peter photographed the five of us
crossing over the start line at 9.45am, only 15 minutes late today. Things
are improving. We then turned round, went back over the start line and
headed along the Cornish Coastal Path in clockwise direction. The sun
was shining, the views were stunning and we all felt very lucky to be
there. Derek really is a game lad. He's only been out of hospital for a
week after a suspected heart attack. He and Sheila walked with us for a
mile or so, bade us farewell until tomorrow evening and then we were on
our own.

We walked through the attractive seaside village of Sennan Cove with
its pleasant harbour and beautiful beach and then took a footpath to avoid
the main road, the A30. I'll tell you something; they're not very good at
maintaining footpaths in Cornwall. A machete would have been very
useful. It was like a jungle. I couldn't get through the undergrowth and
kept having to leap over trailing brambles. Ken tried ploughing a way
through but it wasn't easy for any of us. By the time we emerged at the
first road crossing, less than half a mile away, we were so relieved to be
on tarmac we decided to follow the road instead of the shorter route on
the footpath that we had planned to take. I hope that all the footpaths
aren't like this or it looks like we'll be going the whole way by road.

We got onto the A30 and walked along it for a mile more than we'd
planned to, and it really wasn't a nice road to walk along. We came off
it again and got back onto our planned route, and for most of the rest of
the morning we were on bridle paths and minor roads. Several boots,
socks and insoles juggling stops are made. I ask you, what sort of idiot
would start a walk like this in brand new boots?

We arrived in Penzance closer to two o'clock than the late morning we
had optimistically predicted. We looked a bit of a sight. Kathy had pur-
ple stains round her mouth from all the blackberries she'd nabbed from
the hedgerows and they both looked... well, sort of a mess. No one else
in Penzance had mud on them. It had been fine and dry all day.

As we passed the edge of town we got mixed up with a party of small
school children who thought I was really cute and they all wanted to

.. KATHY HAD TO STRUGGLE AS BEST AS SHE COULD AND NEARLY ENDED UP IN THE ENGLISH CHANNEL.

stroke me. The teachers looked at the 2Ks, all covered in scratches and mud with their rucksacks and a bucket, which said 'Lands End to John O'Groats' on it, and I think they felt really sorry for me. If they looked this dishevelled after only twelve miles, what were they going to look like after nearly a thousand miles?

We walked right down to the sea front and along a bit more of the Cornish Coastal Path, but this time we were going anti-clockwise. I really do worry about their navigation! We've been walking for twelve miles and we're only about two miles further north than when we started. Unfortunately there was some resurfacing work being undertaken on the path and we found ourselves on a building site, but did that stop us? Of course not! We climbed over a digger thing and the man sitting inside having his butties didn't look too pleased. Serves them right, there were no diversion signs and we didn't fancy walking along the main road.

We came to the end of the building site and then we had to wrestle the

.... THE 2K'S ALL COVERED IN SCRATCHES AND MUD .... A PARTY OF SMALL SCHOOL CHILDREN WANTED TO STROKE ME.

barrier to get back onto the footpath. Fortunately, as they were trying to work out how to get me over it, a runner approached and helped lift me over but Kathy, who like me, has legs that were too short to climb over and, unlike me, isn't light enough to be lifted over, had to struggle as best she could and nearly ended up in the English Channel.

We met up with Peter and the van in a car park that looks over to St Michael's Mount, a granite crag half a mile off the coast, which is accessible by a causeway at low tide and by ferry at high tide. The building has been a priory as well as a fortress and a private house and was given to the National Trust in 1957. 15th century fishermen dedicated it to St Michael after claims of sightings of the saint.

They scoffed a Cornish pasty, refilled the thermos with coffee, stuffed a couple of bananas and a Mars bar each in their bag and headed north at last. We stopped by the Butterfly Farm at Fraddam and when they'd finished their snack they walked off, leaving the map hanging on a post. What twits I'm walking with! Luckily, they soon missed it and didn't have to walk back too far but they really will have to get their act together if we're ever going to get to John O'Groats.

By the time we got to Cambourne it was half past seven, dark and raining. There were no camp sites but a helpful lady at the police station had told Peter of a suitable place to camp, unofficially. We were too tired to take decisions on eating but as we pulled in, low and behold, it was full of inky caps which are edible toadstools, and which, together with a slice of bacon each, some cheese toasties and rounded off with jam and clotted cream scones we had acquired earlier, fed them all handsomely. There were four scones and only three people. Guess who had the other one?

TARMAC TROUBLE
Monday, 23 October, Day Two, 22 miles
Cambourne to Indian Queens on the A30, A3047, minor roads and footpaths.

After a good night's sleep we returned to the spot where we had been picked up in Cambourne, about a mile away. Each time we finish walking at the end of a day we touch a post and when we set off again the following day we touch the same post again. We got out of the van and a chap approached us. "Are you the Trimmers?" he inquired. He was a friend of the afore mentioned Pete Denby called, Tom Smith. He posed with us to touch the post, took some video of us and then walked all through Cambourne pointing out places of interest.

He proudly showed us a statue of Cambourne's most famous son, Richard Trevithick who was born there in 1771. He invented the 'Puffin Devil' the world's first high pressure steam carriage and passenger carrying road locomotive. It took its first passengers from where the statue now stands up Cambourne Hill on Christmas Eve, 1801. Tom invited us to his home for coffee but we felt we must get a move on so we declined his kind offer.

We set off on the A3047 for the first six miles. It really wasn't very enjoyable. I got fractious and the 2Ks got fractious, first with each other and then with me. Ken doesn't think we're making fast enough progress. Kathy moans, first about one foot, then the other, then about her leg. None of us are used to walking on tarmac and it's taking its toll on us already. Do you know how many combinations of foot cover you can make with two different thicknesses of socks, boot liners, and insoles? They have four feet between them to keep swapping and changing. I have four feet to myself and I come ready soled, thank goodness. They certainly couldn't afford to sole me as well. Their footwear and socks cost over £300.

We managed to get off the main road but have to rejoin it again just after Redruth. Redruth was once the capital of the largest and richest metalliferous mining area in Britain but now bears the scars of industrial decline. We eventually get off the main road and there is a choice of minor roads or footpaths but after yesterday's experience we think we might stay on roads.

The tarmac gets more painful so we change our minds and decide to look at the footpaths. Thank goodness we did. We walk most of the remainder of the morning on well-maintained bridle paths and footpaths. I am off my lead and we are all happy again. We pass lots of remains of 18th century tin mines. These sites have been recently short-listed for World Heritage Site status, which will rank Cornwall's mining history alongside Stonehenge and the Pyramids.

Just before we met Peter for lunch, we joined the dreaded A30 trunk road. To get onto it we should have followed a bridle path but, just before it joined the A30, it turned into a replica of the footpath yesterday morning and we still hadn't acquired a machete. We nipped into a potato field, over a bramble hedge and slid down a bank onto the road verge. Not the most elegant way to join a major trunk road but then we don't care too much for trunk roads. Our parting the A30, later on in the day, was no more stylish. We were desperate to get on to the minor road through the village of Mitchel and were horrified to find there was no access to it until the far side of the village, which meant an extra half a mile of hell for us.

We couldn't bear the A30 a moment longer so we hopped over the parapet and slid down the bank at the spot where the minor road went under the A30. A man on a road-cleaning vehicle was just coming under the A30 on the minor road and gave us a very strange look. Perhaps he thought we were going to ask for political asylum. How the likes of Ian Botham and our friends George Jones, Ivan and Alan managed to walk the whole route along main roads beggars' belief. We found it very hard and found no pleasure in it at all.

The last three miles to Indian Queens was sheer heaven. We were on lovely minor roads, which were no more than farm tracks. They were typical Cornish roads, sort of sunken lanes really with a bank, a wall on top and high hedges that almost formed a tunnel. We met Peter who picked us up and took us to Derek's house at Mevagissey where I got my dinner and a sleep and they got their dinner and what Kathy described as the best bath she ever had.

RUNNING DOWN - AND UP
Tuesday, 24 October, Day Three, 24 miles
Indian Queens to St Breward on footpaths, lane, the dreaded A30 and the Camel Way

We wanted to see Mevagissey in daylight, so we had a leisurely breakfast. They had cereals, toast and some more of Sheila's jam. Derek would have liked to produce the full works for them but they really find it hard walking on a full stomach and have forewarned all our hosts so that people don't stock up on sausage and bacon especially for them. After a fond farewell to Derek we drove back to Indian Queens. It should be all back lanes and footpaths today. We turned off down a footpath and it was like the jungle bits on the first day. We still haven't managed to acquire a machete so Ken pressed his Swiss Army penknife into action. It got worse. Cornwall County Council will be receiving a bill from us for footpath maintenance. Eventually we managed to get off the footpath and onto a farm track.

We're into running downhill on tarmac. We don't run fast but running actually changes the way we land on our feet so that we put pressure in different places and we use different muscles in our legs. We were so relieved to be back onto the road that we even ran up hill. We were so busy running we forgot to concentrate on the map and ended up back on the dreaded A30, only for a mile and a bit, but were all gibbering wrecks again. We eventually worked out a system: one K in front, me behind with the other K on the outside of me, and me, pulling on my lead and acting neurotic. We move along at great speed with a tail wind, almost dragged along by the pantechnicons.

We're soon back on the lovely lanes and for the next eight miles to Bodmin we don't see more than a dozen vehicles. Peter is quite surprised to see us so early; we've done about thirteen miles, including the jungle bit, in not much more than four hours. A quick lunch and we're on the move again, along the Camel Way, which is a footpath on an old railway line. This bit should be easy... except that we see a sign pointing the wrong way, and the river was running the wrong way. So we took out a compass for the first time so far, and that was pointing the wrong way too. About turn! I ask you, what chance have we got of ever finding our way to John O'Groats if they can't find their way along a railway line? Someone put a donation in our bucket but it's a wonder they didn't ask for it back when they saw us going back in the opposite direction.

Four miles further along there was an ice cream shop. The kind lady had heard about us on the wireless and donated the cost of the ice cream to our fund. She also told us that the footpath was closed further on and we'd have to take the road all the way to St Breward. We ended up on a road that did an awful lot of ups and downs. And then we saw St Breward - up on top of a hill.

Peter and the van (not the wolf) were waiting for us and we parked just up the road from the pub on the edge of Bodmin Moor. Hope the beast isn't on the prowl tonight. Reported sightings of the beast suggest that it could be a big cat, such as a black panther, possibly released when the 1976 Dangerous Wild Animals Act was passed. A Government investigation was carried out in 1990 and they decided that it didn't exist, but in 1999 the RAF were still looking for it.

The lovely A30

Dinner and early bed for me; they went to the pub, rang logistics (Mollie) as they did every night to report our progress and also rang Radio Cornwall. We have had a couple of mentions on the wireless and people are looking out for us so we rang to thank them and let them know that a man, his dog, his wife and a Rainbow Trust collecting bucket were making good progress. They ate at he pub but weren't late back. They must be getting old!

BODMIN, BOGS BUT NO BEAST

Wednesday, 25 October, Day Four, 22 miles

St Breward to Lifton, crossing Bodmin Moor then on minor roads and one mile on the A30

We inadvertently heard the weather forecast last night - rain and gale force winds. We avoid weather forecasts if we can. They're seldom right but unfortunately for once they are right and we spend a rocky night in the camper van on the edge of the moor, wondering what the famous Bodmin bogs will be like tomorrow. We're away by eight o'clock for what could be one of the hardest days of the walk, crossing Bodmin Moor. The 2Ks are adorned in waterproofs from head to foot. I am in the same coat I wore, day and night, for the whole journey.

We set off at pace, past lots of signs warning us that it is private property. They really don't like people crossing the moor and not without reason. It could be quite a dangerous place to be if you don't have good navigations skills. We were taking a bit of a risk really but it was a far more direct route than following the minor roads and we definitely didn't want to cross it on the A30.

The access on and off the moor is on tracks but there is a bit in the middle which is no man's land and it is seriously boggy. We took a compass bearing and headed off into the mist. Eventually we came to a rocky outcrop with a bit of gorse to provided shelter and they had a biscuit and a banana each to keep their energy level up. The mist lifted a little and do you know what we saw? The enemy without - the dreaded A30! We've avoided it so far today and now we can see it, but it can't see us, so we have the advantage! We find the track and we're off the moor by mid-day. The 2Ks are far better at navigation when there are no roads to lead them astray.

We came off the moor at the tiny hamlet of Codda and took a legal bridal path over more moor to Trewint, which has been bypassed by the A30. We then took a minor road to Polyphant. All this complicated navigation saved us about 20 miles of the dreaded A30. We had to walk along it for about a mile just after Polyphant but we were soon off it again and on to minor roads for the rest of the day.

On the little bit we had to walk along, one or two motorists gave us a pip when they saw our bucket and us. It seems we've had another mention on the wireless. Two miles beyond Launceston we cross the River Tamar and into Devon and a born again Christian postman gives us a donation and implores us to read St John Chapter three. When we return to the camper van we tell Peter that it's one of his jobs, along with cleaning the van every time we get out of it.

Poor Peter, they treat him just like Cinderella. Anyway he refuses, using the fact that he is a Buddhist as an excuse. We continue on to

Lifton where they find a garage that has a sideline in Cornish pasties so they buy three, hoping they will meet up with Peter before his goes cold. They'd just got back on the road when the van appeared. Good old Peter!

We're on a proper camp site tonight but the facilities aren't very good. They could do with a decent plumber. Kathy rustles up something out of the esky and Ken and Peter go to ring logistics. They're gone a long time. I think the 'phone must be in the pub.

FAREWELL, A30
Thursday, 26 October, Day Five, 28 miles
Lifton to North Tawton and beyond on minor roads and footpaths

We drove back to last night's finishing point and set off at a pace and by the time we meet up with Peter at a quarter to twelve we'd done about fifteen miles, including kissing the A30 goodbye. It was all lovely minor roads. We passed through the villages of Portgate, Lewdown and Bridestow. The weather was lovely and we were all feeling really good. A mile or so beyond Bridestow we joined the A30 where the A836 crosses over it. We walked along it for no more than half a mile and then headed along the B3260 to Oakhampton.

We have wonderful views of Dartmoor to the south. It would have been nice to take a more southerly route and cross over the edge of the moor but when we took a close look at the map, it seemed that most of it was marked as a 'danger area' and we weren't too sure about the access to it. It's a crying shame that many of the most beautiful parts of our wonderful island are littered with bits of ammunition, and we're still doing it! We met up with Peter just before Oakhampton, got in the van for a quick bite and guess what? It started raining. Perhaps the 'born again' postman has had a word with his boss because we seem to miss all the wet weather.

We saw a group of about half a dozen ramblers today. You should have seen the gear they were wearing. Looked like they were off to the North Pole and there's the 2Ks, walking a thousand miles in T-shirts which is all they've worn for the whole walk so far, except for the first mile or so each day and the bit across Bodmin Moor yesterday. We walked on for a further seven miles to North Tawton, which should be our destination tonight. With the exception of the last mile into North

Tawton when we joined the Talka trail, it's all on a minor road but it's too busy for me to be off my lead so we just plod on, not really enjoying it too much.

We got to North Tawton for about half past three and decided to walk on a further six miles towards Lapford. Wow, that's 28 miles and we finished walking by half past five. The last six miles were quite pleasant because there was hardly and traffic and I was off my lead. Peter has found us somewhere to camp in a caravan sales park. There is no one there, just a lot of empty caravans and us. They're off to the pub to eat tonight, the White Hart at Bow.

The landlady cooked them beautiful fish and chips and when they ask for a doggy bag to take the lovely salad away that they couldn't manage, conversation is steered to why we're in a camper van, what we're doing and the charity were doing it for. She tells us that she has had personal experience of the sort of situations that Rainbow Trust provides support for; she has lost a child to cancer. It is a poignant moment.

POORLY FOOT

Friday, 27 October, Day Six, 27 miles
Just before Lapford to Westleigh on minor roads and the Grand Western Canal

Another early start and we're through Lapford before it's rubbed the bed out of its eyes and manage to miss Witheridge due to yet another lack of concentration on the map. It's not a big problem, we just end up in Nomansland (honest!) and take a slightly different route and meet up with Peter for lunch at Calverleigh two miles before Tiverton, which should have been tonight's destination.

After lunch I'm reluctant to get moving. My right front paw doesn't want to go. Peter hangs around in case it gets worse but after a few minutes I'm walking fine so he sets off to pick up some shopping in Tiverton and go about nine miles further on to find a camp site. We catch a glimpse of him in Tiverton as we're walking through the town centre. What a lovely place it looks.

We continue on through Halberton and then get on to the Grand Western Canal. It was lovely to be off the road at last. This was our first stretch of canal and if they're all as nice as this we should really enjoy the two hundred miles we intend to walk on them. After about another five miles we see Peter waiting for us on a bridge, looking relieved to have found us. It's twenty past six by then and starting to get dark. We're quite tired, having walked 27 miles today and 55 over the last two days, but we are now nine miles ahead of schedule and feeling very pleased with ourselves.

We are trying to get ahead of schedule because the day after tomorrow we have a 29 mile day walking to Cheddar and that has now been reduced down to about 20 miles, providing we have another good day tomorrow. The camp site we intended camping in is closed and the only other one Peter has discovered that is open is quite expensive. The 2Ks eyes light up. If it's expensive they probably have good facilities.

They get to the camp site and cough up £12.50. "I hope the showers are clean," Kathy comments. The lady says she'd send her daughter, who was paid to keep them clean, to check them out. Kathy went in to see if there was anywhere to do some washing and had to clean the washbasins before she could wash her socks in them. Half an hour later the daughter, a thirteen-year-old, turned up. Kathy told her she'd already done the washbasins and would be claiming part of her wages. The girl then squirted a bottle of something on the floor, flicked a mop round and said some rather rude words about cleaning toilets and off she went. How do these people get away with it?

They cooked dinner in the van, Kathy went off to ring logistics and I went to bed. I have definitely damaged my right foot and I'm not walking tomorrow which means I will not be getting myself into the *Guinness Book of Records* as the first dog to walk Lands End to John O'Groats for charity.

The trouble is that I can't tell them how I feel about walking every day so they have to err on the side of caution. The big problem is that Peter will be leaving us the day after tomorrow and if they don't think I'm up to walking I will have to go back home in the van. Much as they don't want to send me home, they don't want to put me under pressure.

My Day Off

Saturday, 28 October, Day Seven, 27 miles

Westleigh to just past Bridgewater 27 miles on minor roads and the Taunton & Bridgewater Canal

Peter was rattling the van, demanding to get off the site at 6.30am. He hadn't had a good night. The 2Ks were so tired they didn't hear the noise on the camp site but it had kept Peter awake all night. He had heard one woman use the 'F' word four times in one sentence and it had offended his delicate ears. Anyway, he got in the driving seat; drove back to where we had been picked up last evening, opened the door and threw them out. And it was still dark. It was only just gone seven o'clock.

Do I know when to take a day off? For the first time on the walk it rained really hard. I stayed with Peter all day and we were real heroes, being at the appointed place both for our lunchtime meeting and at the end of the day. We had dropped them off back on the Grand Western Canal which they followed almost to the end and then left it on a minor road, headed towards Wellington on the A30 and crossed the county boundary from Devon to Somerset. They skirted round Wellington, which I'm sure, is a lovely place even if we didn't see much of it. They were soon off the main road and back onto minor roads again, following the route of the M5 but far enough away for it not to be a problem.

We met up with the 2Ks at about one o'clock, and they were absolutely soaking, but still amazingly cheerful. They had had a reasonably good day, having walked about sixteen miles so far, mostly on 'A' roads but it hadn't been quite such an ordeal without me. The worst bit had been through Taunton, which they reckoned was more dangerous and more difficult to navigate than Bodmin Moor. They had then joined the Taunton to Bridgewater Canal for most of the rest of the day and, although it really did rain hard they were fairly sheltered.

They set off to walk a further ten miles to just the other side of Bridgewater. Another good thing about following canals is that the navigation is easy, except that Kathy spied a footpath on the map which avoided following the canal all the way into the centre of Bridgewater and saved about a mile or so walking along a road out of Bridgewater. The only problem was that it went under the M5 and there was a railway line and the River Parrett involved and the map was a bit hazy as to where the footpath actually crossed the river and how.

A 'suck it and see' decision was made and they discovered that the footpath actually went under the motorway and attached itself to the side of the railway line to cross over the river. Good old Ordnance Survey maps! They're our very best friends. Most people walking Lands End to John O'Groats do it all from a road atlas. We were fortunate in buying almost all the maps we needed at half price from a friend of a friend who bought the maps and then decided not do the walk. You need about 35 in total, at about £6 each it can add up to quite a lot. They love looking at maps and always buy maps of where they're going before they get

THE GIRL THEN SQUIRTED A BOTTLE OF SOMETHING ON THE FLOOR, FLICKED A MOP ROUND AND SAID SOME RATHER RUDE WORDS AND OFF SHE WENT!

there if they can. They're also wonderful things to look back on after a holiday, better than photographs in many ways.

Back to the walk - by the time they had finished today they were about fourteen miles ahead of schedule and had walked 175 miles in seven days and felt pretty pleased with themselves. We met them with wonderful news. We had found a superb camp site with excellent facilities including a laundry. The owner had said that we could put the fee of £12 for the three of them in our collecting box. When Kathy saw the toilet block she thought it was her birthday, thirteen loos, six showers and fourteen washbasins, all spanking clean and all to herself. We seem to be the only people on the camp site.

They rustle up a meal out of the esky, shower, sort out the washing, phone logistics and go to bed. Tomorrow should be an easy day. We're only about fifteen miles from Cheddar instead of the 29 we should be if

... 13 LOOS, 6 SHOWERS AND 14 WASHBASINS,
ALL SPANKING CLEAN AND ALL TO HERSELF.

we hadn't managed to get so far ahead of schedule. We'll hopefully walk another couple of miles further on past Cheddar to the top of Cheddar Gorge tomorrow but that's all. From the following evening we are being picked up by different people each night so there is no point in being ahead of schedule. I do hope I'm all right walking tomorrow. It will really put the dampers on things if I have to go home with Peter on Monday.

FEELING BETTER

Sunday, 29 October, Day Eight, 17 miles
Bridgewater to the top of Cheddar Gorge on minor roads and footpaths

I'm up early chasing rabbits around the camp site. The clocks went back an hour last night. We set off at about seven thirty, which is really eight thirty, if you see what I mean. Peter dropped us off about a mile down the road where they finished last night, then returned to the camp site to take his tent down and meet us about ten miles further on. It's a lovely walk, crossing over the drains south of Cheddar. We met a few people out walking dogs and one of them put his hand in his trouser pocket and gave us a £5 donation. Surprising how much money people take with them when walking the dog!

We met up with Peter at about eleven o'clock at the lovely village of Blackford and he had also received £5 from someone who had stopped to chat to him whilst he was waiting for us. We're soon off again, this time on a 'B' road and we become entwined with a load of runners on a 10k road race. They are quite surprised to find a man, his dog, his wife and his bucket jogging along amongst them. We're offered honourary membership of their running club and receive many interesting comments. 'How many more miles have you got to do?" asked one lady. We told her we'd got about 760. "I've only got one and I think that's one too many." she replied.

Many apologised for not having money on them for our bucket. We thanked them for their generous good wishes and really meant it. Money isn't what matters or why we carry our bucket. We carry it to make people aware of the charity and let people know what we are doing.

We turned off the main road to walk along a track and met up with two walkers, a middle aged couple. They ask about the charity and also give us a £5 donation. People are amazingly generous. We really don't expect donations. Good wishes is quite sufficient, perhaps a bit of loose change if they have some to spare.

Just after one o'clock we met up with Peter who had found a camp site about a mile out of the village, (yes, Cheddar is a village). We walked into Cheddar and Peter drove us to the camp site, as it isn't on our route. We then had a massive sort out in the van as Peter is going home tomorrow and the 2Ks will have to carry all their clobber. They have to decide how little they can exist on for the next eight or nine days. It took a couple of hours and then they drove back to the village to walk up the Gorge.

It started raining and they saw little point in getting me wet, so they left me in the van and the three of them walked up the Gorge, found the footpath that they will take over the top tomorrow, and then walked down it again, into the wind. They were all wet through by the time they got back to the van. We went back to the camp site and they had showers in the wonderful en-suite facilities. Again we seem to be the only people on the site. The owner doesn't want any payment as we're on a charity walk and the facilities are as good as last night, absolutely perfect.

The 2Ks have decided they will take Peter out for dinner tonight. So they should. He has been at every appointed pick up point twice a day for more than a week, tidied the van and washed up every time they have left it, mostly looking like a bomb site and he has happily slept in his tiny tent every night whilst we have wallowed in luxury in the van.

Cheddar has plenty of tea rooms but is a little short of restaurants. They find a good Indian and walk in, in all their wet gear, hoping some of it will dry out while they are eating their meal. Kathy wants to dry her socks over the thing they put on the table to keep the food warm but is over-ruled. The waiter is interested in their T-shirts and the story of the walk comes out. He proudly shakes the hands of the heroes congratulates them on their achievement so far and wishes them well for the rest of the walk.

As they say, it's not about money; it's about the warmth of the good wishes they are getting. It makes the walking easy, even when they're cold, wet and tired. A quick ring to logistics and off to bed for the last time in the van for about three weeks.

THEY FIND A GOOD INDIAN AND WALK IN ALL
THEIR WET GEAR... KATHY WANTS TO DRY HER
SOCKS, BUT IS OVER-RULED!

FLOODS, HAIL, THUNDER AND LIGHTING
Monday, 30 October, Day Nine, 32 miles
Just past Cheddar to Severn Bridge, nearly all on roads

We've discovered a problem. It seems we have miscalculated the distance from Cheddar to Severn Bridge. Originally we were going to walk to the Avon Bridge, which is 22 miles. We changed our plans because we had an offer of accommodation for tonight and Severn Bridge was a more convenient pick up point but we forgot to recalculate the distance and Severn Bridge is eight miles further on. And that isn't the only problem, not by a long way! It has rained really hard all night. Poor Peter hardly had any sleep. He thought he was sleeping on a water-bed.

He was up bright and early and drove us, in the dark, up Cheddar Gorge to where they finished walking yesterday afternoon. There are rocks on the road that have fallen off the cliff face and the water cascading down the road was hitting them, then shooting up into the air like fountains. Peter stopped by the footpath that we should have taken from the road, and it's not there, there is a stream, well, a raging torrent there instead. We looked at the map. To divert round by the road will add a couple of miles to our already excessively long day, but it's hardly worth

Avon Bridge - M5

THE WIND WAS SO STRONG IT WAS IMPOSSIBLE
FOR THEM TO CYCLE INTO IT.

the risk of trying to get along the footpath. We got out of the van and off we went. It was wet and dark.

Peter met up with us about six miles further on. He'd been listening to the radio. Apparently the country is in chaos. The M25 is closed because of flooding; there are hardly any trains running and they have snow in Staffordshire. The M6 and the A66 are closed, also because of snow and most of the West Country is flooded.

I am cold and wet and stressed out from walking along the road and they decide to leave me in the van to drive to the next meeting point about ten miles further on. Peter and me drive off, straight into a deep flood. Peter backs up to the 2Ks. 'Get in the van' he demands. They reluctantly do as they're told and Peter drives them through the flood, not more than a few yards but Kathy is quite upset about accepting a lift. "Do you want kill yourself?" enquires Peter.

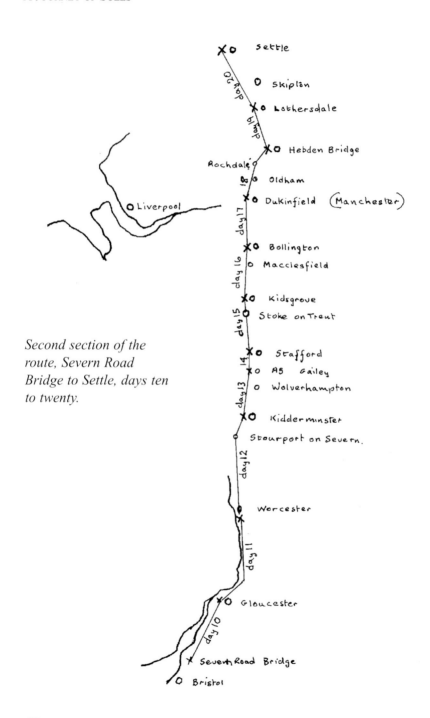

Second section of the route, Severn Road Bridge to Settle, days ten to twenty.

THE SECOND BIT - BY KATHY

Monday, 30 October, Day Nine
Continued

As Ken and I battled on through more floods, we had a discussion about Ranger. She wasn't happy, the traffic made her stressful and if this extreme weather continued, as it was forecast to do, we might have to use roads more often than we had planned to. She would be getting cold and wet and we really didn't think we were being fair on her. We decided we would ask Peter to take her home. We met up with Peter again at about one o'clock for lunch and told him of our decision. He agreed, Ranger looked miserable, her tail was hanging down and was still shivering from this morning's drenching. She is also still moulting and dogs are never at their best when they're moulting.

We ran on again, through hail, thunder and lightening but feeling a lot happier. We had left our camera in the van because we were afraid it would get wet. It was a pity, because we came through the village of Felton and it was white over with hailstones, looking just like a Christmas card. People caught out on their way to the village shop had to take refuge from the hail wherever they could. One man dived into the telephone box and others into a bus shelter.

People gave us strange looks but we just ran on, the wind pushing us from behind. I was checking the map without stopping and my foot went into what appeared to be just a small puddle and the next thing I knew I was on the floor. The puddle was actually a hole full of water and it was more than a foot deep. With the wind blowing us along and, without Ranger we were better able to tolerate the main roads. We had a little respite from them, along a pretty footpath by a stream for a mile or so, but then we were back through the industrial area around Avon Bridge.

The bridge takes the M5 over the Avon and is over a mile long. We walked over the cycle way that is separated from the motorway by quite a sturdy barrier - thank goodness. Again we were being blown along by the wind so it wasn't too bad but would have been hell trying to go the opposite way. Cyclists coming towards us were pushing their bikes. The wind was so strong it was impossible for them to cycle into it

We had a major road intersection to cross just after the bridge and we just took our lives in our hands and ran through gaps in the traffic when we could find them. Peter drove on for a further ten miles. He is supposed to be going home today but refuses to leave until he has seen us safely delivered into the hands of David and Margaret Woodall who have offered to put us up tonight.

There was a time when we all thought we weren't going to make it all the way to Severn Bridge. We see the Welsh mountains across the Severn Estuary and the new Severn Bridge in the distance. We are meeting David and Margaret, former walking holiday guests, by the old Severn Bridge, which is a few miles further on, at 5.00pm. We crossed over the two Motorway links to the new Severn Bridge and finally arrive and the meeting point at about a quarter to five. All was quiet, as the bridge was closed due to the high winds. Our van and David and Margaret's car were the only two vehicles there.

While they were waiting for us a security man had been to both vehicles and aimed his electronic device at their number plates and told them that if they were still there in two hours they would be fined. Peter explained why they were there. The man said he didn't care why they were there, rules were rules. Good old Granada Services! For heavens sake, they were the only two vehicles in the car park.

When we arrived we changed into some clean clothes, stuffed all our dirty clothes into the van for Mollie to wash and said farewell to Peter and Ranger. They both looked tired and we felt they would both be better off at home. Peter had done a wonderful and quite thankless job. Ranger simply needed to be in familiar surroundings. The walking wasn't a problem but she just looked scared when there was heavy traffic around. We knew she would be better off staying with Mollie and Mollie's dog, her best friend Fudge.

If we could have stuck to our original plans and stayed off the roads, and if the weather hadn't been so extreme, she would perhaps have been all right, but there are still a lot of main roads that can't be avoided and our schedule seems to be too tight to allow for too much relaxation for any of us. It took about half an hour for David and Margaret to drive us back to their house at Wotton-under-Edge, passing through Thornbury on the way. They both appeared to be nice places.

We arrived at the house and were shown into a lovely room. Unpacking doesn't take a long time when you're carrying as little as we were. We each had one pair of very light trousers, a fleece jacket each, one set of spare smalls, a couple of T-shirts and long sleeved tops which were communal, a very small emergency kit, a torch, a deodorant which was also communal and a toothbrush. We did think of sawing the end of our toothbrushes to make them lighter but it never quite came to that.

We had a pair of shoes each that would have been strong enough to walk in for a few miles had we had a disaster with our boots. I discovered that mine would fit inside Ken's so he carried the shoes and I carried our packed lunches. Our waterproofs fitted on the top of Ken's rucksack but the bucket fitted on the back of my bag better than on Ken's, so I had the bucket and Ken had the map case on the back of his rucksack when we weren't using it. It had a card saying 'Lands End to John O'Groats for Rainbow Trust' visible on the outside and our bucket said the same in large letters so people could see what we were doing.

Ken also carried the other maps we needed to get us back to Cold Keld. As we were going to be walking mostly on canals for the next part of the journey we had the relevant Nicholson Canal Guides with us. We planned to leave maps that were finished with people along the way so Ken's load will get lighter.

Our intention is to invite all our host families to Cold Keld for a weekend sometime soon and people can return them to us then. We had our first bath for a week. Sheer ecstasy! Showers are fine if you just want to get clean but there is nothing like wallowing in a bath to soothe aching muscles. We then rang logistics and told Mollie that Ranger was on her way home.

People have been so generous in offering us hospitality. We had a lovely meal and a look at the map for tomorrow's walk. We want to be out on the road by seven again tomorrow and we have to drive back to where we finished today. As we had had quite a tough day, both emotionally and physically, we felt quite tired so we made our excuses and climbed into our first real bed for a week for another early night. It was like climbing into heaven!

KNEE DEEP IN FLOOD WATER

Tuesday, 31 October, Day Ten, 25 miles

Severn Bridge to Tuffley, 3 miles west of Gloucester, on the Severn Way and the A38

Margaret and David drove us back to our finishing point last night and walked with us, in lovely sunshine, for the first mile or so from Severn Bridge. We are on the Severn Way, a long distance footpath that follows the River Severn. We know that we won't be able to stick to our original plan which was to follow the River Severn to Sharpness and then follow the Gloucester & Sharpness Canal, as we saw on the news last night the river has burst it's banks further on.

The bit we are walking this morning is on a raised dyke so we are okay but we know that there could be trouble ahead with the flood waters from yesterday's downpour. We could see floods on the Severn Way ahead of us so decided to come off the footpath at Berkley Power Station and

Severn Bridge with David and Margaret Woodall

.... HER SHEEP ARE ON A SMALL GRASS MOUND ...

headed towards Berkley village to join the A38. The track was in an enclosed lane, two feet deep in water. There was a thick hedge at one side and the high perimeter fence of the power station at the other side so we had no choice but to walk through it. At least our trousers and boots were clean when we emerged at the other end!

In Berkley, we saw where the flood had risen to yesterday. It was about three feet higher than today. Yesterday we would have had to swim down the lane. A lady stopped us to put money in our bucket. "If you'd been here yesterday we would have taken you through the village by boat," she told us. They're really nice people in Berkley but I wondered how our sponsors would feel if we'd have accepted a lift in a boat! I'm still feeling guilty about going through that bit of flood yesterday in the van.

Our hosts tonight are Pete and Kate Ellis, more former walking holiday guests. About half a dozen miles from Tuffley we find Kate and her lovely spaniel Jim waiting in a bus shelter. Kate had left her car at tonight's finishing point and come on the bus out to meet us. It was lovely to see her and know that we had no worries about finding our bed for tonight. Kate was a wonderful guide and took us through the rather built up area around Tuffley, which is a suburb of Gloucester. Thank goodness she did. I think we would have struggled a bit on our own.

We passed lots of very new and very large out of town shops, almost like American style shopping malls. Again we struggled to cross over road intersections. These places are designed for motorists, not walkers. We walked back to Kate's car and it was just a few minutes drive to her house. We had another luxurious bath and Kate's husband Pete arrived home to join us for a delectable dinner. We have known Pete and Kate for quite some time but this was the first time we have visited them at their home. We weren't as tired tonight as we had been last night and it was lovely to share a relaxing evening with friends.

FLOODS, BUT NO WET FEET
Wednesday, 1 November, Day Eleven, 27 miles
3 miles south of Gloucester to 3 miles south of Worcester, all on the A38

Pete has to leave for work early so it's no trouble for him to drop us off at our finishing point last evening. We're off by 7.30am and Kate has the day off work and guides us through Gloucester, passing the docks and then the Cathedral where she meets her friend the Dean. We should have asked him about St John Chapter Three. We still haven't read it. It was wonderful to be guided by someone with local knowledge and we are able to enjoy the sights of Gloucester instead of spending all our time with our nose pressed against the map.

I am fascinated by the expressions, or lack of expression, on people's faces as they sit in their cars in the traffic jams, as they no doubt do every morning. Many were eating their breakfast, or using their mobile phones, or both. One lady had a phone in one hand, a pen in the other and was steering through the slow moving traffic with her elbow.

I try smiling at some of them and a few smile back, but mostly they look away. Probably think I'm some sort of weirdo, just because I'm walking through Gloucester with a rucksack and a bucket attached to it. I reckon the most miserable looking people were the ones in the most expensive cars. I know without a shadow of doubt there was not one of them who would want to change places with me and that there was not one of them that I would want to change places with.

We walked along for a while with a rather athletic looking lady who had just taken her children to school and was interested in our walk. She would have liked to do what we were doing. She apologised for not having any money on her to put in our bucket. We thanked her for her good wishes and told her that was worth more than money.

I always kept a few sponsorship forms in my pocket to give to people that took an interest in what we were doing, and many people were. They would ask how long we had been walking, where we were heading for that night, what route we were taking, what date we were to finish and such like. The little yellow forms had lots of information, including our itinerary and daily mileage, as well as information about Rainbow Trust.

Many people had heard of Rainbow Trust, a lot knew vaguely that it is a children's charity. By giving people one of our forms we were spreading the word about the charity. Carrying the bucket made us far more visible than just carrying a small collecting box. It wasn't too much trouble and it came in handy as a seat and for putting bits and bobs in, but I couldn't really run with it if it had anything in it.

We needed to run occasionally, not necessarily to get somewhere quickly but to alter the pressure on our feet and legs. I found walking on tarmac all day made my feet ache. It is often possible to find a bit of grass verge and although it slows us up we use it whenever there is any. We will have to be on tarmac all day again tomorrow as there is no chance that the flood water will recede for another couple of days.

The day after tomorrow we will be on the canal and that should be okay. Canals don't usually flood because they are really drains and all the surplus water drains into the rivers and out onto the flood plains. Anyway, that is what should happen and we live in hope. It would be lovely to feel something more forgiving under our feet and be away from the traffic at last. Although we're still missing Ranger, we have no regrets about sending her home. We're both more relaxed now that we don't have to keep taking her needs into consideration.

We said a fond farewell to Kate who left us mid-morning to get the bus back to Gloucester. We stopped around mid-day to eat the butties she had supplied and there was a car drama happening across the road. A lady had broken down, a gentleman came along in a very expensive look-ing sports car to help, but the lady's car wouldn't start and they needed an extra hand to push. He came over, introduced himself and asked Ken to help. His face looked vaguely familiar and we think he might have been someone famous, a football manager or something, but neither of us could remember who he said he was. Anyway he put a generous donation in our bucket.

We had quite a leisurely day today so we went into a coffee shop by Tewkesbury Abbey. The man gave us a funny look when we arrived with rucksacks and buckets but was very friendly when he realised we were on a charity walk and didn't charge us for the two cups of coffee we each had. He gave us one of his cards with a good wishes message on. We also had a donation from another lady in the coffee shop who had driven past us earlier this morning.

Now the free coffee leaves me in a moral dilemma. Had we paid for the coffee and he put the money in our bucket, the charity would have benefited and as we have said we are paying all our own expenses, we should really put the money in the bucket. By the same token, should we be putting seventy or eighty pounds a night into the bucket for all the free beds and meals we are being given? It looks like we won't be paying for beds for more than two or three nights on the whole of the journey. I dismiss the whole issue from my mind. Morality is far too complicated. Anyway, this morning, amongst the disgusting litter on the road verge, Ken found £1.60 and that went into the box. Coffee paid for from gutter. That's fine!

The Severn Way

We plodded on and crossed from Gloucestershire to Worcestershire, past lots of floods but managed to keep out of them. We saw signs to the footpath we should have been on, the Severn Way. It was completely submerged. A five bar gate by the sign had only the top visible. We got to the pub where our host for tonight, Cicely Harrel was to pick us up, to find it is surrounded by flood water. It was on an island! We had an offer from a friendly farmer's wife to take us there by tractor but there was no point, as Cicely wouldn't be able to get there. The farmer's wife pointed out her sheep to us. They are on a small grass mound sticking out of the water just beyond the pub. I hope they're safe because the water seems to be rising rather than receding.

We found a telephone box and Ken went to telephone Cicely. While Ken was in the telephone box I chatted to the farmer's wife. I don't know why I refer to her as the farmer's wife and not the farmer. I suppose it has to do with her age, somewhere vaguely over seventy, of an age when it was acceptable to be 'a wife', to give support to your husband and bring up your children yourself. Anyway, she told us about a few of the Lands End to John O'Groats walkers she'd seen pass through and pointed out a seat outside her house where Dr Barbara Moore had stopped to rest in 1962.

Ken returned from the phone box. Cicely had left work early because she worked on the opposite side of the river and she knew she wouldn't be able to get home if she left at her normal time. She suggested that we continued to walk towards Worcester and she would drive out of Worcester along the same road until we met. It was getting dark and we watched the sunset over the Malvern Hills. The weather had been beautiful all day. Not a drop of rain had fallen on us for two days so it seemed silly that the flood water was still rising. We quickened our pace to get further on and out of danger. The tide had now turned and we could almost see the water rising in the fields and lapping over the edge of the road.

It took Cicely almost an hour to travel the seven miles from her house to where she picked us up. The roads were in chaos and it was announced that the bridge in Worcester will close this evening. There is a threat of the worst flooding for seventy years due to a combination of a high tide and water running down from the hills. We got to Cicely's house and put the telly on. The whole of the Severn valley may be flooded tomorrow and it's all Tony Blair's fault!

Now you won't hear me say much in defence of politicians but I don't think that the blame for all the water running down from the Welsh hills and hitting against the high tides in the Severn Estuary can be entirely placed at the feet on Tony Blair. Perhaps the other bloke, William Haig, do they call him? might be able to have some impact on the situation. If he is in a pub somewhere in the Welsh mountains consuming fourteen pints at a session and then going outside for a long piddle then we might be able to pin some of the blame on him, but not Tony Blair.

Thank goodness Cicely's house is quite high up. Cicely produced a lovely meal and later we were joined by a friend called Diana who had just been to hockey practice. When a hockey player and a clog dancer meet there is bound to be good crack. We had a jolly evening.

GRIDLOCKED

Thursday, 2 November, Day Twelve, 18 miles

3 miles South of Worcester to Kidderminster on the A38 and the Stafford and Worcester Canal

We listened to the local radio. 'Don't try to go anywhere today' they advised. The bridge in Worcester is closed, everyone is trying to get round the ring road and the whole place is grid locked and there is worse still to come with the floods. Great, we are seven miles away from where we finished walking last night and there doesn't seem to be any way of getting back, short of walking seven miles south, turning round and then continuing on our way. We don't really want to do that.

Cicely sees no problem at all. If we can get on to the M5 motorway three miles north of Worcester, head south for twelve miles, get onto the M50, head west then we can get back onto the A38 and head north to where she picked us up last night. All very simple! I cringe with embarrassment at putting anyone to this much trouble. Cicely insists that it won't be any trouble at all as she has a meeting this morning and when she drops us off she will just continue on her way. However she packs an overnight bag just in case she can't get home again.

We do all the motorway bits and we're heading north up the A38 when we get to the place where we should have finished yesterday and we are diverted off the road as it is completely submerged. My thoughts turn to the farmer's wife and her sheep and I hope the bit of high ground she had them on is still above water. We eventually get back onto the A38 and Cicely drops us off at the point where she picked us up. What a hero! By now its twenty minutes to ten. We're meeting our hosts for this evening in a pub about nine miles away at 12.30pm. With a bit of luck we should be there just about right.

We walk past the cathedral and I try to take a photo of it. It looks depressing with scaffolding round it, almost as if it is also trying to shelter from the rain. It's all very miserable but I'm cheered when a lady stops me to put money in our bucket. We plod on and find a bus shelter where we eat the butties Cicely has provided us with, and the sun came out. There was a lovely rainbow, the first we've seen for a few days.

It reminds us of the charity and my thoughts drift back to last week and the lady at the pub at Bow. She said that one of the hardest things when her child was dying in hospital was seeing parents take other children home when they were cured of their illness; being genially happy for them and knowing that she would never take her child home. "I just wanted a room to go and scream in," she had told me.

If some of the money people are generously donating can provide something as simple and as necessary as somewhere for a distraught parent to have a scream, then it will be money well spent. She also told me that her child had been lent to her for a few short and precious years and loosing him had made her a different, and she thought, a better person.

We arrived at the appointed meeting point, the Kings Arms at Ombersley to find ten members of Bromsgrove Ramblers, all former guests on our walking holidays arriving in cars at the same time. We're dragged, kicking and screaming into the pub and a pint of the local brew is forced into our unwilling hands. Someone informs 'mien host' that he has a pair of intrepid heroes on the premises and he forces £10 into our collecting box. We spent a convivial twenty minutes in there, during which time Cicely appeared with our map case which we'd left in her car. Twits!

As we were leaving two ladies who were having a meal called me over to their table. They had driven past us along the road and wanted to know about our walk. Another £10 went into the bucket. We set off to walk the nine miles to Kidderminster, back along the A38 and discovered we have left all our maps and map case in the pub. If that map case reaches John O'Groats it will be a miracle!

Fortunately Bromsgrove Ramblers are well equipped with maps and

... WE'RE DRAGGED, KICKING AND SCREAMING INTO THE PUB....

some of the group will be returning to the pub car park at the end of the walk and can retrieve our map case then. We find a route off the A38, through the village of Stourport on Severn to the canal towpath which means we will be on our planned route for the first time for three days. The road in Stourport is flooded, but not too deep.

A policeman is directing the traffic and we manage to get round the flood without too much trouble. I was at the back at this stage and a very large HGV stopped in the middle of the road as he drove out of the flood water, called me over and dropped a handful of change into the bucket. Everyone else stopped and gave him a big round of applause. It was quite a scene.

I was too busy wondering what the policeman was thinking to notice too much but all the other girls in the group were drooling. They all want a bucket now so that they can attract big handsome hunky lorry drivers. We're frog marched along the canal to Kidderminster and through the town where we pass one of only three remaining carpet mills left in Kidderminster. Kidderminster is famous for carpet manufacturing and, in it's heyday, had more than thirty carpet mills.

We finished at the railway station where the couple we are staying with tonight, Janet and John Ingram had left their car. Other people are ferried back to the pub where we all met up and one of the group promises to retrieve our map case and bring it along tonight when we're all meeting at another pub for a meal.

We were driven back to Janet and John's home and have a cup of coffee while we watched the news on the telly. Things are getting worse. The whole country is in chaos because of the floods. The Severn Valley and the River Ouse are the worst affected. We bathe and the it's just a short walk down to the pub where we meet up with the rest of the group again and about fourteen of us sit down to a wonderful roast dinner, washed down with a few pints of the local brew. Unfortunately, or perhaps fortunately the beer pumps ran dry, otherwise there would have been some very sore heads the next day.

A FULL DAY OF CANAL NAVIGATION

Friday, 3 November, Day Thirteen, 26 miles

Kidderminster to 5 miles north of Wolverhampton

After a lovely breakfast and a look round their beautiful garden, John drops us off at Kidderminster Railway Station where we finished yesterday. We find our way through the town and we're soon back on the canal. It is a delight. We are feeling on top of the world and each step is pure pleasure. All feet problems are now behind us and we bounce along. I feel that I have never been fitter in my life. I'm not the athletic type but I do have a fair bit of staying power and although I found the walking tough for the first few days I am really enjoying it now. Ken is stronger and fitter than me and I occasionally have to remind him that my legs are a lot shorter than his.

We still do a bit of running, even though there are no hills to run down

on the canals. Our feet feel so much better now that we are on the canal tow paths. The paths are mostly gravel but there is often the option of walking on grass it we fancy a change Squirrels and a great assortment of birds entertain us. I see an electric blue flash, a kingfisher darting across the towpath in front of us. We stop for a short break to eat the butties that Janet provided us with. A friendly robin sits by our side and is delighted to find a crumb I had dropped. Our resting spot is a seat dedicated to Jim Robbins who was the chairman of the Staffs and Worcester Canal Society from 1964 to 1967. It has the following inscription:

> 'O commemorate me with no hero-courageous tomb,
> Just a canal-bank seat for the passer by.'

We thank him for his hospitality and continue on our way. The next building is called Nail Maker's Cottage, which reminds us of Kidderminster's other traditional industry. Women in an outbuilding of their homes mostly did nail making. They would slice the wire at an angle to make a point and then flatten the head.

Walking along the canal is a delight, not a single bit of industrial backyards that most canals seem to be blighted with. Each lock or bridge brings something new to feast our eyes on. Quite a lot of the canal is cut into the bare rock. The river follows it quite closely, catching the spare water that runs away in the unique circular over spill ducts. We tramp happily on our way and the only slight niggle is that we have forgotten to stock up on chocolates. We find a Mars bar or something similar gives us all the energy we need. We are actually finding we don't need a lot to eat and don't feel hungry but if we don't have something sweet we start to feel tired. We keep hoping to see a canal side shop but none appear. We eventually see a sign to a shop and I leave my rucksack and bucket to go and find it. It's nearly a mile away from the canal and up a hill. We won't make this mistake again. By the time I got back to Ken I'd been away for almost half an hour.

We meet a boat coming through a lock and a lady puts £5 in our bucket, which puts an extra spring in our step at the end of a long day. Tonight, son Adam, who lives in Stafford is picking us up. There seems to be a bit of confusion about the pick up point. He spends an hour waiting in a pub and we spend an hour waiting on a dual carriageway half a mile down the road. It's the first time our pick up has failed and we feel a bit cross. Eventually Adam turns up and takes us to his home. He goes off to a bonfire celebration with wife Louisa and our grandchildren Victoria and Mary and we have a nice bath, watch the telly and have a nice relaxing evening.

POOR BEGGARS

Saturday, 4 November, Day Fourteen, 17 miles
5 miles North of Wolverhampton to Stafford on the Staffs & Worcester Canal

Louisa drops us off at yesterday's finishing point at nine o'clock. The weather is fine and sunny and although the canal is still nice, it lacks some of the charm of yesterday's stretch. There is a fishing competition due to start at 10.45am and all the fishermen are setting up their stalls. The equipment they have is incredible and I ask one chap what happened to the man with the wicker basket and the bicycle. A mobile phone rings. "Is that the fish checking your position," inquires Ken.

I ask one of them if he minds me photographing him with all his clobber. "That's fine," he says, "as long as you don't tell my wife what it costs." They all have really long poles so that they are fishing on the opposite side of the canal from where they're sitting. I look in one chap's bag.

"You could set up a plumbing business with that lot," I comment. "Too expensive for plumbing" he says, "two thousand pounds a time just for the poles." One man puts a few coins in our bucket.

"Thanks, best of luck. May the best equipment win," we say as we leave them sorting out maggots and all the other things that are necessary for a good day's competitive fishing.

We stop to eat butties about mid-day, by which time we'd walked about ten miles. We have a permit for a street collection in Stafford but we're not allowed to start until 4.00pm as another charity is collecting there today.

We dawdled on but still got to Stafford before 2.00pm. We went into a cafe to kill time. The plan was to do the collection and the walk back to Adam and Louisa's house so that we could start from there tomorrow and save anyone having to drive us to our starting point. We just couldn't think of a way of killing two hours so we walked on the mile or so from the town centre to Adam and Louisa's home, thinking we might possibly ask them to drive us back later.

To be quite honest, we're not good at begging. We're happy to carry our bucket, let people know what we're doing and accept donations if they want to give them to us, but the thought of two of us standing in Stafford expecting people to give us money was not too appealing. We'd originally thought we would have Ranger with us. Her big soft eyes, her Rainbow ribbons on her collar, and a notice on her back saying she was walking from Lands End to John O'Groats would have been very appealing but us two standing there on our own with a bucket. In the end we didn't bother. We promised to make a better effort the following Saturday when we had a permit for a collection in Settle and will hopefully have a few other people to help.

We feel a wee bit guilty about it. We also feel a wee bit down. We did a lot yesterday and we needed to do more today. Tomorrow we will have more of a challenge and we're ready for it. We feel like caged animals in a town. Ken spent most of the afternoon playing with the grandchildren and I spent most of the afternoon writing. It is my way of unwinding when I'm tired or frustrated. We had a nice meal with all the family and went to bed listening to fireworks outside. Bonfire Night seems to be a three day celebration in Stafford.

THE DAY I LOST KEN

Sunday, 5 November, Day Fifteen, 30 miles
Stafford to Kidsgrove on the Trent & Mersey Canal

We're away by twenty minutes past eight; bit later than we should have been. A cyclist stopped to give us a donation. We thank him, both for the donation and taking the trouble to stop. He replied that seeing us was an excellent reason to stop for a bit of respite from peddling hard up a long climb and well worth the cost of the donation so it seems we've done him a favour and he's done us one. We joined the Trent and Mersey Canal about three miles north east of Stafford where it crosses under the Uttoxiter road.

We've arranged to meet a group of artists from Bolton who have stayed at Cold Keld several times in the last few years. We are meeting them at Stone at about eleven o'clock. We reckon it's about nine miles so we crack the pace on. Again the walking is delightful and we think about Ranger and how she would have enjoyed it.

We got to the first bridge on the outskirts of Stone at about 10.30am. No sign of the group so I left Ken by the canal with the bags and popped up the road to find a loo. I couldn't see one so I popped into a supermarket to see if they had one. It was like being in a science fiction film! I'd not been in a shop, apart from small village shops since before we left home and it was huge and bright and had big brash signs hanging from high ceilings so they could be seen above all the high shelves. I felt quite scared. It was weird.

I came out and found a sign pointing back to the canal by a different route and I thought I would follow it as it would rejoin the canal further along and I might just meet up with the group. It did rejoin the canal, but about a mile and a half further along, and then I had to run back down the canal to Ken who had been sat wondering where I was for the best part of an hour.

As I was running back along the canal I passed our friends, about half a dozen of them. They were rather surprised when I ran past them going southbound. I was in too much of a panic about losing Ken, and worried that he would be worrying about me, to stop and explain in detail why I was on my own and going the wrong way.

"Would you like to borrow a compass?" one of them yelled.

Eventually we all got together and had an enjoyable walk for a mile or two. It really is lovely to keep meeting up with people and adds extra interest to our days. They all adjourned to the pub for lunch and we continued on our own, heading towards Stoke on Trent. I have always described Stoke on Trent as the place I hate most in the whole of England. I have yet to find my way through it by road without getting lost. Someone told me that the secret is to remember that the centre of Stoke on Trent is called Hanley, and that Hanley isn't one of the 'five towns', so heaven knows what it is. And from the road it looks a real dump. Now most places that look okay by road look like a bomb-site from the canal - try navigating the canals through Manchester.

Stoke on Trent by canal is a delight. There are wonderful plaques telling the history, the towpath is beautifully maintained and we saw virtually no litter. Next time I have to go through Stoke on Trent I am definitely going by boat. It was a real pleasure. Three miles from the end of today's destination is Harecastle Tunnel. As we approach the tunnel it starts to drizzle and we don our waterproofs for the first time since

Worcester, three days ago.

We have been so lucky with the weather. The wind is still at our backs and we have had seen the sun almost every day so far. We come to the tunnel, which is nearly two miles long. It doesn't have a towpath through it so we have to go over the top. It's not as simple as it seems, especially in the fading light. We end up in a gypsy camp site and a very helpful man points out the way. We eventually get back onto the canal in the centre of Kidsgrove. Kidsgrove was originally a big iron and coal production town and was helped in its prosperity by the completion of the Trent & Mersey Canal.

Our meeting point with our host for the next two nights, Muriel Timewell, is another half mile or so. We come off the Trent & Mersey Canal at Hardings Wood Junction and cross over Red Bull Aqueduct, which carries the Macclesfield Canal over the Trent & Mersey Canal. We stop to marvel at the wonderful feat of engineering. It's almost dark by now and we inadvertently end up in a boat yard. Ken soon sorts the problem out and we reach the meeting point just after 5.00pm.

Muriel is yet another former waking holiday guest. It's only about a four-mile drive to her lovely home at Alsger. She picked us up at Red Bull Junction, which is the junction of the Trent & Mersey and the

Red Bull Aqueduct - the Trent & Mersey Canal meets the Macclesfield Canal.

Macclesfield Canal. We had a gorgeous soak in the bath, another lovely meal and caught up on news. She has a lovely dog called Curiosity and, since we last saw her, she has managed to fulfil a dream that she has had for over forty years - she has acquired her own horse. She proudly shows us a picture of her horse, which is called Magic, in the way that most people of her age show pictures of their grandchildren. In the picture she is sat astride her handsome steed, the smile on her face almost wider than her helmet and she looks like a teenager. We have another early night, as we are quite tired. I think it has a bit to do with the fact that it gets dark so early now and walking in fading light always seems more tiring.

WE'RE ALL EARLY!
Monday, 6 November, Day Sixteen, 20 miles
Kidsgrove to 4 miles north of Macclesfield, all on the Macclesfield Canal

It rained all night and the four mile journey back to our finishing point last evening takes almost an hour because of diversions round floods. Muriel is determined to get us back to the same place as she picked us up from but it is impractical. It would involve driving right through the 'five towns'. I'm feeling very benevolent towards Stoke on Trent and I don't want to see it from the road and I definitely don't want to get lost in it. We persuade Muriel to drop us off and we find our way through a housing estate and get back to last night's finishing point on the canal by twenty minutes to ten.

We are meeting my sister Peggy and a dear friend of hers, Albert Vaughan, a sprightly 89-year-old who wants to walk part of the way with us. They both live near Mansfield, my birthplace and home for the first 35 years of my life. I describe it as a good place to come from. Albert has friends in Congleton, hence the meeting there.

We jog quite a bit to make up for lost time. Because we are going back to Muriel's house tonight we don't have to carry all our clobber. Ken has his bag, with the bucket attached to it. I just have the map. Jogging is a lot easier without a rucksack and we find ourselves in Congleton early. We step off the canal by the aqueduct that carries the canal over the A527 with ten minutes to spare before our one o'clock meeting time. We find a seat conveniently placed for us, sit down to eat our butties and Peggy and Albert arrive. We're all early!

Albert had been in touch with the local press and was disappointed that they weren't here as well. I wasn't too surprised. Can you imagine what the odds were of someone keeping an appointment on time when they had 380-mile walk to get there? Anyway, their office is only a quarter of a mile down the road so we walked down and got ourselves interviewed and photographed walking down the main street.

We went into a cafe for hot chocolate and then got on our way leaving Peggy and Albert to settle the bill. They met us about a mile down the road. When Peggy was paying the bill she got chatting to the lovely waitress and discovered that she used to live in the same road and they had friends in common. Small world!

We walked the next three miles by road, Peggy and Albert stopping every mile or so to take photographs. We felt like stars! After they departed we still had about ten miles left and we ran a fair bit of it. We are feeling really fit but I think we will find it a bit harder tomorrow when we have all our clobber on our backs again.

At precisely ten minutes to five we came up a 'roving bridge' to find Muriel at the top of it, having just arrived there for our five o'clock meeting time. Roving bridges are where the canal towpath changes from one side of the canal to the other and were built in a beautiful curved formation so that the large boat horses could cross from one side of the canal to the other without having to untie the tow rope from the boat or go round any sharp corners.

Anyway there was Muriel, spot on, waiting for us. The drive back to her house is over twenty miles but Muriel is quite unconcerned, despite having been to work all day. Again she serves us a lovely meal and we spend an evening of good conversation, hearing tales of her

Photograph courtesy Congleton Chronicle.

childhood and about Uncle Fred, who married late, had a good war, a diamond solitaire ring and a parrot that didn't talk but was an exceedingly good listener.

MANCHESTER BY THE PRETTY ROUTE

Tuesday, 7 November, Day Seventeen, 20 miles

Bollington to Dukinfield (Manchester) by the Middlewood Trail and the High Peak Canal

We're away from Muriel's by 7.30am but the traffic is appaling and it takes us until nine o'clock to get back to last night's finishing point. Muriel is completely unconcerned. She is delighted to have helped us on our way and has seen it as an honour to be involved in our great adventure rather that a burden. We bid her farewell and feel guilty about her having to wrestle back home through the traffic and then having to go to work. She is a star!

We decided to walk down the disused railway line, which has been made into a footpath and bridle path and is called the Middlewood Trail. It is a real delight and although it doesn't have quite the interest as walking the canal it makes a pleasant change for a few miles. We came off the railway line and rejoined the canal by a lovely, if rather muddy footpath that took us through a heavenly bit of woodland. The weather isn't too good. It's more of an intermittent drizzle than rain but we have our jackets on all day.

Tonight we are staying in Manchester with Rachel who I have known since she was a twinkle in her daddy's eye. Her parents, life-long friends Sue and Graham Kirk, along with my sister Peggy, are driving from Mansfield and are going to park their car at our finishing point and walk back along the canal towpath to meet us and then drive us over to Rachel's house.

Due to a combination of them being late because of the traffic chaos that the floods are still causing and us being early because we jogged quite a lot to avoid walking through the less palatial parts of Manchester in the dark, we were about 300 yards from our destination when we met them. They could at least still have the honour of saying they walked part of the Lands End to John O'Groats walk with us, even if it was such a short distance. We finished by the new Portland Basin Museum and spent an enjoyable hour in there before driving the seven miles to Rachel's house where we all had a lovely meal together.

As Graham has just been appointed a magistrate, we thought he would be a suitable person to oversee us emptying our collecting box. We had last emptied it in Cheddar just a week ago and Peter had taken the contents of almost £50 home with him for Mollie to bank. The last week had added almost £100 and this was entrusted to my sister to bank. We are quite pleased with this and think it is well worth carrying our bucket for. There has not been a single day so far when someone hasn't put something in it. Graham, Sue and Peggy departed at about 10.00pm for their 60 miles drive home. It is so lovely that so many people are putting in so much effort to help us along. It gives us a warm, glowing feeling every time we see a familiar face.

PERFECT TIMING

Wednesday, 8 November, Day eighteen, 23 miles

Dukinfield to Hebden Bridge. 5 miles on the A627, 5 miles on the A671 and 13 miles on the (mostly unnavigable) Rochdale Canal

We finally managed to contact our host for the next two nights this morning. She is Maureen Ludlam, chairman of Hebden Bridge Ramblers Group and she has arranged a press call for us, and members of her group at 2.00pm in Todmorden - eighteen miles away. Fortunately we don't have too much trouble with the traffic and are back to our starting point and away by eight o'clock. We set off walking up the road. Ken has a puzzled look on his face.

"Are you sure this is the right road?" I ask. "I think so," he replies, stroking his beard. I can always tell if Ken is unsure about something because he strokes his beard. I don't know how I could tell when he was unsure of things before he grew a beard. "Have you got a compass handy?" I ask.

He takes it out of his pocket and sure enough we are going the wrong way. We are walking east and the road we should be on, the Oldham Road, goes due north. About turn. That's the first time we've used a compass since Bodmin Moor. I suppose we would look strange to people on their way to work but a compass really is an essential piece of equipment for us. We never go anywhere without one.

We have ten miles on road through one of the less opulent areas of Manchester. The road is going due north and is a very convenient link between the Macclesfield Canal and the Rochdale Canal so we grit our teeth and get on with it. We pass a butcher's shop and can't resist calling in for a pork pie, even though Rachel has provided us with a more than adequate packed lunch. The lady assistant can hardly believe what we are doing, and puts a donation in our bucket.

We walk through Oldham, Royton and the outskirts of Rochdale and the shops we pass are a depressing array of betting shops, sandwich bars, tanning studios, hairdressers and newsagents advertising every sort of scratch card and other 'get rich quick' schemes. The other thing that keeps catching our attention as we travel through the country is how many used cars are crammed on every garage forecourt. The country

.... A COMPASS REALLY IS AN ESSENTIAL PIECE OF EQUIPMENT FOR US. WE NEVER GO ANYWHERE WITHOUT ONE !

seems to be awash with unwanted second hand cars.

We're delighted that we manage to cover the ten miles of road in two and a half hours. There is a bit of a drizzle and we have our jackets on all morning. The rain is actually an asset because we find tarmac is less painful to walk on if it's wet. It was lovely to find ourselves back on a canal towpath. The first few miles of the canal are un-navigable, but there is restoration work in progress. The first part was completely covered in vegetation and full of rubbish but further along there was work being carried out on restoring the locks and one section was drained and we were amazed at the depth of it.

In two places bridges have been replaced with new ones that aren't navigable and the canal just flows through small culverts. There will be major works to rebuild them to allow for navigation to link it back to the main canal system in Manchester. We finally get to the part that is navigable, and very soon we are approaching Todmorden. All we know is we will be met on the canal at 2.00pm but the problem is that the canal weaves it's way for nearly two miles through Todmorden and we're not sure where we are to meet them. We look ahead and see a church ahead of us. We keep walking towards it, the clock strikes two and our friends step off a bridge onto the towpath in front of us. They arrived, we arrived and the clock struck two. Not bad when we'd walked eighteen miles to get there.

We were taken up to the main street and more of the group appeared until there were about a dozen. The press reporter and photographer appeared, interviewed us and then took photographs of them presenting us with a cheque of our funds. We then all set off together to walk the five miles to Hebden Bridge. It seemed to take no time at all in such good company. Members of the group pointed out places of interest to us. We passed the confluence of Hebden Water and the River Calder, which is the old Yorkshire and Lancashire border. There is a bridge and the side that faces into Lancashire has a face carved on it and it is know locally as the Stony Stare. I wonder why?

We all paused by one of the locks to remember the family of Lyndsey Riner, a thirteen-year-old girl who's body was discovered in the lock six years ago this week and who's killer has still not been found. There are posters in a lot of the shops, hoping someone might have information that could help find the killer. The whole issue of bereaved parents floods into my mind and I think about the parents of little Sarah Payne whose killer still hasn't been found.

I asked Maureen if there had been any news about the two girls who had been swept away in a river in Stainforth in the Yorkshire Dales just before we started our walk. The first body had been found the day after it happened and she told us that the second body has been found whilst we have been on our walk.

We reach the Hebden Bridge Alternative Energy Centre and three of the party are leaving us here, including John who is celebrating his 81st birthday today. We give him a rendition in traditional style. The rest of the party proceeded to Maureen's house for afternoon tea including crumpets and honey. Yummy. Everyone departed; we had a lovely soak in the bath and a delicious meal.

WONDERFUL WIDE OPEN SPACE

Thursday, 9 November, Day Nineteen, 18 miles

Hebden Bridge to Lothersdale on permissible paths, the Pennine Way and open fell

We were off at about 8.30am and, as we're coming back to Hebden Bridge tonight we don't need to carry all our clobber. Maureen had said she would take our collecting box to work and there seems little point in carrying the bucket over the fell as we're not very likely to meet anyone. We climb, quite steeply at first to Wandsworth Fell. We are on a permissive path across a heather clad grouse moor. It takes us down to Walshaw Dean Reservoir where we join the Pennine Way.

We climb up again to 448 meters, the highest point of our walk so far. I reflect back to the same time yesterday when we were walking up the Oldham Road. It might as well be a different planet. The day wasn't bright but it was fine and dry. I kept looking for photographic opportunities but nothing I could get into the view-finder could capture the day. It was perfect. I think we had been so hungry for the wild open spaces we are more familiar with. We had forgotten what it felt like.

Devon and Cornwall had their charm and we found the sea and estuary view stunning. The canals had their interesting architecture and there were always waterfowl and boats to add interest. The roads were a nightmare but still had their interest in the fact that we saw lots of people and we were always receiving donations and words of encouragement but

what we saw today is what walkers dreams are made of.

We followed the Pennine Way and climbed up another ridge and came down into the Worth Valley, pausing at 'Top Withins' of *Wuthering Heights* fame where we eat our lunch. We've eaten lunch here before, over ten years ago when we walked the Pennine Way. Then we were loaded down with camping gear and it was a lot harder under foot. Most of the path is now paved which makes the walking just all pleasure. The slabs are all rough so they don't get slimy and dangerous and they protect the delicate environment.

I remember my first ever encounter with the Pennine Way. I was about eight-years-old so it must have been about 1955, before the whole of the route had been legally defined. We were a family of five and it was our first camping holiday. We didn't have a car or a tent, but we managed to borrowed a tent. A friend of the family, a man called Billy, drove us to Edale, the starting point of the Pennine Way, in his van on a Saturday morning, promising to pick us up in a week's time. It was lovely when we got there but within an hour or two the cloud came right down to base level and we never saw the view again. It rained, constantly and with attitude! The cows had to pass our tent twice a day on their way to the milking parlour, and by Saturday night the grass outside the tent was like a quagmire.

We had taken a tin chest in which we kept all our clothes and also doubled as a table. We may have been from the council estate but we had standards and we weren't going to let them slip, especially on holiday! The only problem was that every time we had the table laid, complete with a tablecloth of course, someone wanted something out of the chest.

The farm where we were camping supplied milk but we hadn't realised that it didn't come in bottles, so we set off to walk the mile or so to Edale in pursuit of a milk jug. We didn't manage to buy a milk jug but I do remember my father pointing to a footpath sign, which said 'Pennine Way'. "That footpath goes all the way to Scotland," he told me. I desperately wanted to walk it, there and then. I'd never been to a foreign country.

Over thirty years later I got to walk the Pennine Way. We backpacked with Ranger's predecessor another Labrador bitch called Rover and a tent, Ken carrying more than his share of our clobber. Sadly my father had died a couple of years before, but I'm sure when we left Edale at the start of our journey I heard him say, "Go on our Kathleen, you can do it now."

Back to the milk jug, the shop in Edale hadn't got one, so we set off to walk to Castleton. We were so exhausted by the time we got there that we had to have a taxi back. When we returned to the tent, cows had invaded it, most of our food was gone and all our money had been spent on the taxi. By Monday we had run out of dry clothes and had to ring Billy and ask him to come and pick us up again. I remember our mum making us all stand in the river in all our clothes to get the worst of the mud off before Billy came. She didn't want us dirtying his nice clean van. The whole holiday only lasted a weekend but it provided a lifetime of memories.

Back to today, we came down to Pondern, across the dam and were soon climbing up again, over the next ridge and into Cowling. We stopped again and ate the remainder of our lunch, this time by a delightful little footbridge over a stream. Again I spare a thought for all the people who have done Lands End to John O'Groats on the roads and not known the pleasure and relief of getting onto more interesting terrain.

We had a small problem. It was only two o'clock and Maureen wasn't likely to be able to pick us up until after five o'clock. We tried to spin

Above - walking with the pupils of Ravenstonedale School and MP David Maclean, picture courtesty of Cumberland and Westmorland Herald Below - Cornish tin mines (left) and a Cornish lane (right).

Under the M6 near Stafford

Contrasting scenery days 18 and 19.

Dumfries Bridge - old and new

Carrbridge

St. John's Kirk

Loch Fleet - Sutherland

out the last five miles but still arrived at Lothersdale by half past three. There are no shops or cafes and the pub doesn't open until six o'clock. We killed a bit of time in the phone box, ringing our daughter and logistics and then the local radio station. It seems that Mollie has got a feature about the walk on *Fresh AM*, the Yorkshire Dales radio station. It will be going out at four, five and six o'clock. We wandered up the road, wondering how to kill time when a vehicle drew up. It was our friend Pete Denby from Kirkby Stephen who had supplied our walking boots.

He'd had business in Skipton and finished early and decided to come and look for us. He'd followed the track up onto the fell from Cowling, seen two sets of boot prints, one smaller than the other and realised they were probably ours and we were on our way to Lothersdale. It was a real surprise to see him. He already had his car radio tuned into the local radio station so we listened to the feature about us.

It wasn't too long before Maureen appeared to take us back to Hebden Bridge. We had only walked eighteen miles but the drive back must have been almost twice as far. Yesterday Maureen had been explaining that her husband John is learning to play the Northumberland pipes and has a lesson this evening. Maureen was explaining the situation to us and trying, very delicately to explain that John's tutor had a slightly out of the ordinary dress code. "He's called Adrian," I said. She stopped dead in her tracks. "He's a friend of ours," I explained. We got back to Hebden Bridge, Adrian arrived to give John his lesson and was taken aback to find the house full of familiar faces. Maureen was off to choir practice and suggested I went with her and took our collecting box so off we went. When we returned to the house a few other musicians had turned up and there was a lovely informal jam session in full flow. What a lovely evening!

Heading for Home
Friday, 10 November, Day Twenty, 18 Miles
Lothersdale to Settle on and off the Pennine Way

Maureen works in Keighley and has to go to a meeting this morning so dropping us off back at Lothersdale is not a lot of trouble for her and we are walking by half past eight. "Which way are you heading?" she asks. "Up there, to the bottom of the rainbow," Ken replied, pointing to a lovely rainbow. It had obviously been raining earlier but once again we were lucky and didn't see a drop of rain all day.

It's quite a steep climb out of Lothersdale and we set off with the sun on our backs and a spring in our step because today is a red-letter day - we are going to sleep in our own bed tonight. We spend all day flirting with the Pennine Way, using it when it suits our convenience and taking shorter routes at other times.

We passed the rather grand Broughton Hall then crossed over the A59 just before Gargrave where we bought a lovely pork pie to go with the cheese sandwiches that Maureen had given us. The A65 goes through Gargrave and as we were trying to cross it a lady dropped some money in our bucket. "I heard about you on the wireless last night," she told us. Fame at last!

We continued on through Gargrave and crossed the Leeds Liverpool Canal. We looked over the bridge and saw a few boats moored on the wharf. This is a very special place for me. It was on this wharf 30 years ago that I first saw a narrow boat called Periwinkle which I eventually bought to start a canal boat hire business and it was through that business that I met Ken, my perfect sole mate.

To undertake a walk this length with someone, you have to have a lot of patience, caring and understanding for each other. Although Ken is stronger than me, I think we are now both equally fit. Ken has been wonderfully encouraging whenever I've started to flag, which has given me the extra strength when it has been needed.

People had said that they didn't think that they could cope with being with the same person, continuously and sometimes in quite difficult situations for such a long time. The only way we can do it is to pull together. It would be sheer hell to have to do a walk like this with someone you didn't like and I feel sure I couldn't do it on my own. Joined at the hips

Otterburn

we may be, but that suits us both fine.

We continued on up a lane, that eventually becomes a rather rough track. Middle-aged couples coming the other way stop us when they see the bucket and want to know all about the walk. They apologised for not having any money on them but we gave them a form. Who knows, they might send in a donation. We then met up with two other ladies out for a day's walking. We slowed our pace down for about half a mile and enjoyed their company while they quizzed us about our walk and then gave us a donation.

We came down off the track to the village of Otterburn. A man asked where we were walking. When we turned round and he read what it said on our bucket, he asked why we were going this way. "Because it's heading north," we replied. He agreed that it was but couldn't understand why Otterburn was on a direct route from Lands End to John O'Groats. We followed another track called Langber Lane, which we think is probably the original route from Gargrave to Settle. It is a lovely track, if a bit boggy in places. The Woodland Trust owns a lot of the adjoining land. We're amused to pass a ruined building with no roof but a burglar alarm. The nearest tarmac road to it is about three miles away so god knows whom they think the alarm would alert.

Again we made faster than expected progress and arrived in Settle about an hour before Mollie was due to pick us up to take us back to Cold Keld. We're quite anxious to get home and see Ranger and our two cats. Ranger was delighted to see us and looked in really good form, far better than when we last saw her. I still had vivid memories of when she left to go home with Peter and she had looked cold and scared. We will definitely take her with us tomorrow and hope that she might be able to be with us for the rest of the walk, but we will take each day as it comes.

There is a bonfire party tonight in Fell End, the almost non-existent settlement we live in. Bonfire night was postponed in Fell End last weekend because one family had a bereavement and the funeral was on Bonfire night so it was put back a week which also meant that it coincided with our homecoming.

Despite the wind, rain and hail there were several dozen people there, more than half of them children. It took a bit of dousing with petrol to get the fire going but once it took hold it soon became a raging inferno. Several mattresses arrived later to be added to the pile and were used as trampolines for the last hour of their lives. The hot dogs and burgers were sizzled on a bar-b-que and drinks flowed freely. Our neighbours were all keen to hear about our adventure and a good night was had by all. We had had some wonderful hospitality over the last three weeks but there is no bed in the world quite like your own.

I'M BACK - BY RANGER
Saturday, 11 November, Day Twenty-One, 18 miles
Settle to Dent via Ribblehead. On the Pennine Way and the Craven Way

We're doing a street collection in Settle, so it will make for a rather late start. The 'team' is assembled: it includes Mollie, a few friends and a few recruits from Giggleswick School. I try to look cute but we can't hang around too long as we have eighteen miles to walk today. We have company all day as a friend of Mollie's is being sponsored to walk with us today. We're on the road for the first ten miles, and although it is only a minor road there is too much traffic for me to be off my lead and I don't enjoy it too much. We stop for an early break in the church porch at Horton in Ribblesdale. Dedicated to St Oswald, it is a delightful place with its solid looking square tower and friendly interior.

They eat the pork pies they bought in Settle. Okay, but not a patch on the ones from Gargrave yesterday. They seem to have become authorities on pork pies in my absence. When I was last with them they were still in Cornish pastie country. We are following along the line of the Settle-Carlisle railway all morning and the views are lovely. We have a

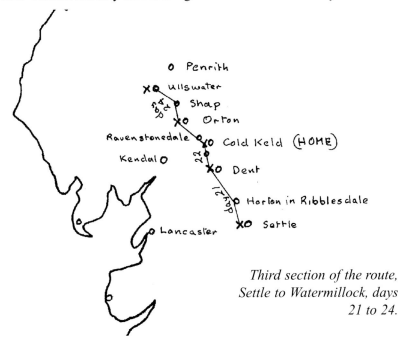

Third section of the route, Settle to Watermillock, days 21 to 24.

light wind at our backs and even see the sun occasionally. They strip down to T-shirts but they now have long sleeved tops as well. There is a definite change in temperature today, but it is fine as long as we keep moving.

We reach the Ribblehead Viaduct just after one o'clock and, bliss, there is a bacon buttie wagon there, which supplied them each with an excellent egg and bacon buttie. There is a pub by the viaduct and outside the pub is a phone box and this reminds the 2Ks of a funny story they once heard in funny situation.

A few years ago they had been away for a weekend cross country skiing at the very remote Loch Ossian Youth Hostel on Rannoch Moor in Scotland. There had been hardly any snow all weekend, but it snowed the night before they left. They were travelling back by car and the snow kept falling. They got to four miles north of Lockerbie and all the traffic had ground to a halt. It snowed all night and nothing moved for over 24 hours. The following day, they actually skied along the M74 to Lockerbie for breakfast. I did tell you they were nutcases didn't I? They spent the night in the car with their two travelling companions, both of whom proved to be incredibly good company and good story tellers, and one of them told the tale of the phone box at Ribblehead.

She had been out, on her own for a few days, cycling in the Yorkshire Dales and had arrived at Ribblehead feeling tired and decided to call it a day and get a train back to home. She had gone into the phone box to check the train times, propping her bike by the wall outside. She made her call, turned round to open the phone box door and realised that she hadn't propped her bike up very carefully and it had slipped down and wedged itself between the phone box door and the wall.

"I was almost in tears," she told us, "I was tired, cold and hungry and stuck in this damned phone box. It took me a full ten minutes to realise the obvious solution; this was a telephone box and there was a telephone in it and I could phone for help." She telephoned the pub.

"You're not going to believe this," she began. She told them of her plight, faces appeared at the pub window and then at the door, her bike was removed and she was released with a great cheer from everyone.

Off we go again, over Blea Moor and this time it's me that finds utopia because I am off my lead for the rest of the day. I find lots of rabbits that need exercise and have a great time chasing about. We're all a lot happier now we're off the road and off we bob, over the aqueduct that carries the river Greta over the railway line.

We follow a well-maintained track, which is part of the Craven Way, up onto the edge of Whernside and reach an altitude of 530 meters, which will be the highest point of our entire walk. We follow the track into a walled lane and soon start on the long decent into Dentdale. The path continues to be well maintained but there are a few places where it is very rough. We catch our first glimpse of the Howgills and really do feel that we're almost home.

When we eventually reached the road, our neighbour Stephen Hopps and son Calum are waiting for us. We explain that we really have to walk all the way into Dent, as that is where we want to start from tomorrow. We are a bit later than we had hoped so they all throw their rucksack into Stephen's Land Rover and run the last couple of miles into Dent.

We're back home again by five o'clock, I get my dinner and they're off to a ceilidh, which the local folk dance club is putting on, the profits from which are being donated to our funds. They have a lovely evening, seeing familiar faces, doing lots of dancing and being treated like heroes for having walked thus far. I'm grateful to have an early night.

MAGIC!
Sunday, 12 November, Day Twenty-two, 12 miles
Dent to Home on roads and the Dales Way

Today was made up of three very emotional events. In the morning they went to our local church, St Oswalds, Ravenstonedale. St Oswalds is a unique church because of the fact that the pews face inwards to the isle and as you walk in you can see everyone's face. They walked in and every single face in the congregation beamed a smile at them. The service today was special for two reasons - one is that it is Remembrance Sunday and the other is that our vicar, Colin Levey is retiring next week. We are a united benefice with Tebay and Orton and Colin will preach his only service on his last working day at Orton

Westmorland Step and Garland Dancers

Church where he lives, therefore this will be the last service at our church. It's not a large congregation but they all feel 'at home' together as they sing familiar hymns.

The names of the 24 people from our village who were killed in the two world wars are read out, as they have been every year for 50 years. Although the 2Ks have only lived in the parish for twenty years, the names are as familiar to them as family. They all stand in silence for two minutes. If only all those two minutes they have stood in our parish church could have give those young men an extra minute of life.

The other unique feature about St Oswalds is its three-tier pulpit and as Colin moves towards it they wonder if he will preach his sermon from the top tier, as this will be his last chance to do so. No, he just preaches from the middle tier. He's a giant of a man anyway, both in body and in character.

Colin has the same opinion as us about war. There is no glory in death, only in life. Over the years he has been our parish priest he has preached some wonderful sermons and many times he has had them rocking in the isles. Today's sermon had no humour but was probably the best sermon they have ever heard. It was also significant that he made no reference to the fact that this was his last service at St Oswalds. The national anthem was sung and the service finished. Then he reminded everyone that there was coffee being served and congratulated our heroes on being there.

The second emotional event was in Dent where we finished our walk last evening. They dashed home, where Kathy changed from her church clothes into her clog dancing clothes because we are meeting the Westmorland Step and Garland Dancers in Dent so they can dance us through Dent. Kathy has been a member of the team for just a year but apparently they had danced for Ian Botham when he walked over Shap a few years before and they wanted to dance for us.

We walked into the pub and there must have been about 40 familiar faces in there, clog dancers, musicians, families and a few friends from the Lakeland Cross Country Ski Club who wanted to walk through Dentdale with us. We had some crack, quaffed a pint and then all assembled outside behind the pub, just as it started to hail. Fortunately it was short lived and there they were, in straw hats and pinnies, musicians playing full pelt, dancing in the street in Dent in November. It was bizarre. Does everyone have friends as eccentric as ours?

They did a couple of dances and while the rest of them did another

Hugh Symonds with the Howgills in the background.

KATHY HAS A QUICK BATH AS SHE IS OFF
TO KENDAL TONIGHT FOR CLOG DANCING
PRACTICE.

one, Kathy quickly whipped off her frock and pinny and put on her
trousers, T-shirt and boots and then we all danced down the road and
out of the village, me between Kathy's legs trying desperately to keep
in step. There were no press there to make us pose, it just happened
and it was magic. We left Dent and the dancers behind and about a
dozen friends joined us to walk the five miles to Sedbergh on the Dales
Way. One was Patrick Higgs, aged seven. He was the youngest person to walk with us. Another was Pauline Symonds, wife of Hugh
who had done the fund raising slide presentation for us back in
September. Hugh was out running from Sedbergh towards Dent and
met up with us and walked back to Sedbergh and two miles further
towards home with us, leaving us for the last five miles on our own.
The weather stayed fine all afternoon and we walked in T-shirts the
whole way. We arrived home in the dark, just after six o'clock.

We're here! The half way mark! The 2Ks had walked from Lands End to home. Whatever happens next, they can at least say that they have walked half the length of Great Britain. Kathy cooked a meal for the first time for three weeks and we had the evening on our own, probably the only evening we'll have on our own for the whole six weeks.

I'm a Star!

Monday, 13 November, Day Twenty-three, 12 miles
Home to Orton on minor roads and the Coast to Coast footpath

Today I am to meet our MP David Maclean in Ravenstonedale at nine o'clock, but first we have to walk three and a half miles from home, as that is where we finished last evening. We set off and as we proceed towards the village many people pass us taking children to school and wish us luck. One car stopped and a man leaned out to say: "You must be the Trimmers. I'm from the *Westmorland Gazette*, see you in the village."

We see a few people as we walk through the village and Kathy stops to talk to a lady who is a reflexologist and a few weeks ago, gave us a cheque for a day's wages when it was national reflexology week. We arrive at the school, which is next door to the church, just as the clock strikes nine, and the press is everywhere. We're introduced to our MP and then pose for all the photographers. All but the youngest of the children at the school are going to walk a couple of miles with us, so we pose for photographs walking down the village with them.

When the photographers had finished we turned around and walked through the churchyard, across the road and head for Park House Farm and the Coast to Coast footpath. There were about 30 children and a dozen or so adults, including the 2Ks' daughter Libby with her dog, my friend Laddie. Another man with a camera charged towards us. "Where's Ranger?" he inquired. I am pointed out and filmed as we walk through the farm. He was from the BBC in Manchester, the same company who had featured us the day before we started the walk.

We continue on and after a couple of miles we said farewell to the children. Peter is waiting with the van, which has now been converted to a mini bus to take the children back to school. All but half a dozen decline the offer and opt to walk back instead. Obviously they're not in any hurry to get back to their lessons.

The 2Ks continue on with two of their dearest friends, Robert and Patricia Hovey from Kendal. Robert was a co-founder of the Lakeland Cross Country Ski Club and both he and Patricia have been on skiing holidays with us as guides for visually impaired skiers.

We are to be met this afternoon by children from Orton school who will walk back for a couple of miles to meet us but we're not meeting them until two o'clock so we have time to kill. The 2Ks know of a tea shop at the garden centre, which makes the best currant and cherry slice in the world and we have to pass it so we pop in. They're on their second cup of coffee when Mollie bursts in looking pretty cross. "I've been looking all over for you, Border TV want to do a feature on you."

What a star I am, two telly companies, four photographers and an MP and it's not even lunch time! Fortunately the telly people are on a deadline so the interview and all the filming take less than an hour and then we're on our way again.

Peter returns after taking the smaller children back to Ravenstonedale and is going to stay with us and bring us back home from Orton. We walk on towards Orton with the Howgills, bathed in sunlight, dominating the skyline to the south. About two miles from Orton we are met by 27 children and half a dozen adults from Orton School. I dash off to greet them, and the children greet me with equal enthusiasm. What a star I've become!

We all walk on to Orton together, the children, glad to be released from school, firing a string of questions at the 2Ks. One child informs them that, by the time they get to Orton they will have walked 501 miles. The 2Ks maths isn't any better that their English, they thought they'd only walked 480. We reach the school and say a fond farewell to the children and promise to go to the school after the walk is finished and tell them about the rest of the walk.

They then head towards the Vicarage where the vicar Colin and his wife Melissa, who are moving to Spain one week from today, have nothing better to do than serve them all coffee. More fond farewells, the next time they will meet is when the 2Ks happen to be passing where they're going to live. Knowing that pair, it won't be too long.

Peter drives them home and Kathy throws a meal together while Ken converts the mini bus back to a camper van as Peter will be returning to join us in about ten days time. Ken loads in all the things that they might need in Scotland, including snow chains and skis. Tomorrow we will be staying at daughter Libby's cottage, which is attached to the Brackenrigg Hotel on Ullswater. Libby is assistant manager at the hotel and tomorrow they are putting on a fund raising event for us.

Kathy opens the mail and there is a cheque from the couple we chatted to when we were walking just past Gargrave four days ago. Pete Denby turned up to sort out about meeting up with us for a day somewhere in Scotland. We have the telly on but our bit isn't on. I hope we haven't been relegated to the cutting room floor!

Kathy has a quick bath as she is off to Kendal tonight for clog dancing practice. It's only a 40 mile round trip: I did tell you she was mad. When she walked in she was treated like a star because apparently the first telly bit we did today was on at lunchtime today. We had missed it!

They could really do with an early night but they have a lot of sorting out to do, making sure all the clothes, bedding and other things they might need up in Scotland are all left ready to go in the van. Kathy gets back from clog dancing announces that she is too tired to think about the packing and promises to get up early in the morning to sort things out.

DAY OF DELIGHT
Tuesday, 14 November, Day Twenty-four, 19 miles
Orton to Watermillock on minor roads, footpaths, fell tracks and bridle paths.

We have agreed to do a telephone interview for Radio Cumbria at 9.20am. The trouble is that it is a bit late for us to do it before we start walking and there isn't a telephone box to call them from between Orton and Shap. It seems that the only solution is to start early and do the interview at Shap. That means that we will have to walk six miles and then ring from Shap in good time for our 9.20am slot.

Fortunately, we have friends at Shap so we will be able to combine our telephone interview with a coffee stop at their house. This is going to be the last time the 2Ks will be at home for three weeks and they have to leave the camper van ready for Peter to bring up to Scotland in about a week's time so things like bedding and clean clothes have to be left where our neighbours can easily find them to load up the van for us. Mollie arrived at 7.00am to drive us back to Orton where we finished last

Daughter Libby at the Brackenrigg Quiz Night

night. We started walking by 7.30am.

As we walk up onto the fell road above Orton a few cars pass us and give us a pip and children yell "Ranger!" as they pass. They must be some of the children who walked with us yesterday. We crossed over the southbound carriageway of the M6 and the minor road we are walking on stays in between the two carriageways for about half a mile. We are sort of walking up the central reservation of the motorway, which is different!

We made excellent time and arrived at our friends Sarah and John's house just after nine o'clock. They rang the radio station and had a coffee and cake while they waited for their interview. They both talk on the wireless. Ken invites the presenter to join us on our walk when we pass the studio in a couple of days time but he declined, miserable thing. When it was Kathy's turn she managed to mention all the things they'd done for the last four days and thank everyone for their support.

We set off again and Sarah walked with us for a short distance. Sarah left us and we seem to be eating up the miles with no effort at all We walked through the lovely village of Bampton and crossed over Askham Fell and into the Lake District on a bridle path from where there is a view of Ullswater with the Brackenrigg Hotel in the distance. The sun was shining and there was a sprinkling of snow on the fell tops.

It was delightful. Sadly we don't have the camera with us to photograph it. The camera we have been using is really Libby's. It is one of these new fangled digital things and Libby took it home with her from Ravenstonedale to download it on to her computer. It's really quite clever. You can store up to about 70 photographs on it and you can see them as soon as you take them and discard the one's you don't want to keep.

Ken pointed out Carrock Fell in the distance but Kathy says she can't see it and even if she could she wouldn't mention it in our book. The track is lovely to walk on and we are quite sad when it starts to descend to Pooley Bridge. We found a shop that sold really good chocolate cake which they enjoyed sitting on a seat overlooking the lake. There were no boats on the move and no one around at all. There can't be many times that you can sit and look at one of Britain's top tourist attractions in sunshine and have it all to yourselves.

We arrived at the Brackenrigg Hotel before half past two and have a pint, which Libby puts on her tab. She's been brought up proper! We then went to her cottage, which adjoins the hotel and had a nice bath and looked at the photographs and she printed some of them out for us. We're really pleased with them.

Libby has arranged a pub quiz, live music, cheap beer and a raffle to raise money for our funds this evening. The pub is sort of not very close to anywhere and this is a Tuesday night in November and when Kathy walked into the bar she couldn't believe her eyes: it's is full of people. Mollie arrived with friends from Leeds and Fell End and the teams assemble for the quiz. Libby's boyfriend, a Geordie with a lovely lilting accent, a twinklie eye and a cheeky smile is the quiz master. Libby refers to him as 'short stuff' because he's not very tall. Talk about kettle calling the pot black, she's even shorter than her mum, who is only about five foot.

After the quiz the band strike up. There are two really good singers, guitar,

Prize winner at the Pub Quiz

fiddle, keyboard and Irish drum and they are really good and they are performing free of charge. The 2Ks are then sent round with raffle tickets and people are queuing up to buy them and to hear about the walk. Libby has printed some of the photographs off on her computer so they show those to people and everyone is very generous in their contributions and have a really good evening.

The 2Ks leave early, about 1.30am but it's about 2.30am before Libby manages to tip everyone out of the bar and get to bed herself. She is up again and back on duty for breakfast next day but never makes any mention of it.

They have decided not to take me for the next bit as they are getting further away from home and if I have any more problems it will mean someone having to drive a long way to fetch me back home again. The trouble is that, like them, I'm a free spirit. I'm no problem out on the fell where I can run free but I can be quite troublesome on a lead. I like to keep stopping to sniff things and I can't do that on a lead. Also they get neurotic about me if there is any traffic around. I'm very sad about it but at least if I stay here with Libby and Laddie I know I'll have good company, good walks and good food, everything I need, except the 2Ks

THE PENULTIMATE BIT BY KATHY
LEAVING RANGER BEHIND
Wednesday, 15 November, Day Twenty-five, 15 miles
Watermillock to Hesket Newmarket on minor roads and footpaths

Libby had returned from her early morning shift at the hotel and was at the computer by the time I rise, printing out photographs from last night's fund raising event for us to take with us when we leave. She counted the proceeds from the raffle and quiz and I re-counted it and filled in a paying in slip for her to pay it into the Rainbow Trust bank account. There is nearly £150, and Mollie took another box containing over £50 back with her so last night we raised about £200.

Libby then made sandwiches for our packed lunch and returned to the hotel to start work again. It's eleven o'clock before we get on the road

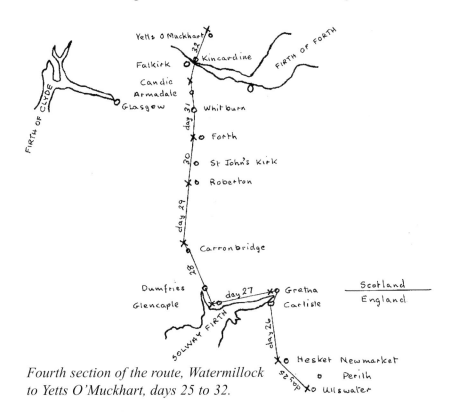

Fourth section of the route, Watermillock to Yetts O'Muckhart, days 25 to 32.

but it is a short day and it's nice to have a more leisurely morning for a change. We feel guilty about leaving Ranger behind and wonder if we are simply taking the easy option. Once she had injured her foot down in Devon we realised that having her with us when we had no back up vehicle was a bit risky. She is a delight to have with us when she can run free but she is quite a liability on the roads. She is still young and perhaps a more mature dog would have coped better. Anyway I give her a big hug and tell her we'll see her again in about ten days time, wipe away the tears and off we go.

We turn our back on Ullswater and head towards the A66 on a very minor road and then on a footpath through a farm. We stop to take photographs of a lovely old signpost that purports to be in Cumberland, a place that ceased to exist about thirty years ago. We cross the A66 without walking along it at all and spend the rest of the day feasting our eyes on the lovely valley of Mungrizedale. The conventional Lands End to John O'Groats route is along the A6, about a dozen miles to the east of

us, no doubt roaring with traffic. Apart from a few tractors we see virtually no traffic at all today.

That was the bit that we walked with our blind friends five years ago when we spent three days guiding them from Carlisle to just north of Lancaster. We have added a few extra miles taking the route we have taken but well worth it, not only for all the free beds we're getting but also for the lovely walking.

We're staying with friends Frank and Rachel Cosgrove at Hesket Newmarket for the next two nights. We walk in T-shirts with our long sleeved shirts underneath all day. There are odd spots of rain in the light southerly breeze and we see a lovely rainbow. Someone has had rain but we manage to keep dry all day. Again!

As we approached the village, we met two men coming over a stile running towards us. One must have been in his early sixties, the other either late sixties or early seventies. They told us that they didn't run too far these days; they were just out on a nine mile run today and asked how far we were walking. When they saw what it said on our bucket they wanted to know about our walk and apologised for not having any money with them to donate.

I thanked them for their good wishes and gave them a sponsorship form so they can keep thinking of us. It was wonderful to meet them and think of the difference between them and the many couch potatoes who sit at home complaining about how the world owes them something better.

We arrived at Frank and Rachel's house, which we know intimately. They bought the house a couple of years ago in a fairly dilapidated state. They spent a year restoring it and employed Ken as their electrician and plumber. At least we know we'll get a decent bath. We sit and have coffee in the spacious kitchen, which has turned out to be everything Frank and Rachel dreamed off. "I want a kitchen with an aga and a sofa," Rachel had said, and that is what she had got. The aga is one of the old cream coloured ones that they had renovated and the kitchen, like the rest of the house is just perfect.

Rachel is intending to walk from her home to Gretna with us tomorrow and gave us a pot containing £105 that she has raised in sponsorship from her friends and neighbours. They have invited a couple of their neighbours, Simon and Sue to join us for dinner. Simon has also worked on the house so we're all old friends. It's a lovely evening with lovely company but I wish people would stop talking about Carrock Fell. I hate it!

WE RAN AWAY TO SCOTLAND

Thursday, 16 November, Day Twenty-six, 23 miles

Hesket Newmarket to Gretna on The Cumbria Way, through Carlisle and over the Solway Firth on the A74

We set off at a quarter past eight and a surprising number of local people seem to pass us on the very minor roads we walk on all morning. We think they are mostly Rachel's sponsors making sure she isn't cheating! The whole of the morning is magnificent and again we have the same weather as we have had for almost all the walk, a light breeze from behind, some cloud and patches of sunshine. We stop by the road in the sunshine to eat the ciabata that Rachel has toasted in the aga.

Carrock Fell is covered in cloud. "Look, it's so awful they've rubbed it out!" I exclaim. We continue on to Carlisle and take advantage of being in the city to buy a back-up battery for the palm-top computer I am using to write my book with. As we are now back to carrying all our own clobber, our packing has been reduced back to more or less what we were carrying in the bit between Severn Bridge and Settle when we were last without a back up vehicle.

My palm-top computer is carefully wrapped in my spare trousers each morning and my camera spends all it's time in the pocket of the trousers that I'm wearing. My spare shoes are tucked inside Ken's spare shoes and my waterproofs are on the top of Ken's rucksack but I carry the packed lunches. The rest of my gear, which amounts to very little, I have in my over-sized bum bag so that I'm not carrying any weight on my shoulders at all.

We seem to be short of a couple of maps so we go into a bookshop to buy them. The bookshop also has a coffee shop in it so I have a lovely hot chocolate and the other two have coffee and cake. We continue on, cross the River Eden and we're surprisingly soon out of the city and after a few rather dull miles through a flat, semi-industrial part we were soon back in rural, if rather flat countryside walking through lovely bits of woodland.

We crossed a minor tributary of the River Eden in the village of Rockcliffe. Just across the river we come to the wonderful sheer rock face from which Rockcliffe very obviously derives its name. A man puts some money in our bucket. I liked Rockcliffe anyway, but I always like places even more when people put money in our bucket. No one was interested in us in Carlisle. People in cities are always too busy.

The next bit was one that we had been dreading: crossing the Solway Firth on the A74. The easiest way to get onto the A74 was to climb over the barrier from the access road and slide down the embankment, so that's what we did. Immediately after it crosses the Solway Firth, the A74 becomes the M74, and most motorists seem to think it is already a motorway and don't expect to see pedestrians walking along the verge. It was awful, traffic roaring past and the verges full of litter. The light was fading fast and we had to concentrate really hard. You could easily damage your ankle on an empty can or bottle. Why do people throw rubbish out of car windows!

We crossed over the River Esk and had hoped to be able to come off the main road and join a minor one that was running parallel with it. We could see the minor road just below us and it was like a quagmire so we continued on the A74 all the way to Gretna, about three miles. It was getting quite dark by now and it was sheer hell! Thank goodness we hadn't got Ranger with us.

We're a bit confused as to where the Scottish Border really is. It has been the River Eden in years passed amongst other rivers. At some time in history it has even been the River Rawthey, near our home. We thought that the River Esk was the border but there is no sign telling us we have crossed into Scotland until we reach Gretna.

We checked the map later and it seems that the channel of the River Esk is the border line all the way along the Solway Firth, but then, instead of following the Esk inland, the border follows a minor tributary of the Esk called the River Sark. It then takes a straight line, slightly south of due east and rejoins the River Esk a few miles further east. We had crossed into Scotland when we crossed the River Sark. You learn something new every day!

It seems the border was sorted when Edward VI succeeded in 1547 and more moderate policies began to be adopted, and action was taken to reinvigorate the "laws of the marches". The first initiative was taken in 1549, jointly by Edward VI, the French king and the Scottish Regent (for Mary Queen of Scots). The treaty dealt with the problem of the Debatable Lands by forbidding nations from either country to settle there. But in 1552, the English and Scottish commissioners finally settled division of the land, with the French ambassador as arbiter. It is called The Scotsdike and runs east and west between the rivers Sark and Esk.

We walked on to Gretna Green where Frank, who had been working all day, picked us up and took us to an Italian restaurant in Carlisle. Rachel then us drove home in his car as he had a meeting and had managed to arrange a lift home with a friend.

When we arrived back we saw Simon, who told us another friend of Frank and Rachel's had heard something about us on the wireless and had collected money from the local art group for our funds, so we arranged to see him in the pub later. In the pub we were again treated like heroes, the landlord standing us a pint of his excellent beer. Hesket Newmarket has its own brewery which a lot of the villagers own shares in so they have a vested interest in drinking there.

I only had a couple of pints tonight but on previous occasions I have attempted to sample a pint from each pump, seven in total. I don't remember whether I have ever succeeded or not but I have always enjoyed trying!!

We have got to know Hesket Newmarket quite well through Frank and Rachel and it is a really lively place but it doesn't have a village hall so a lot of the activities are centred on the pub. A couple of years ago the bar was re-carpeted and the village sign was altered to read, 'Hesket Newcarpet'. The skyline from the village is dominated by Carrock Fell, which I was quite determined not to mention in my book.

The reason I dislike Carrock Fell is that, the one and only occasion I have ever climbed it, was the day after I had had an intensive hydrating session, that time it was at a certain hostelry in Dent, which also has it's own brewery. I was dragged up Carrock Fell, screaming into a hurricane force wind and I didn't enjoy it one little bit. I hate the wind anyway; you might have noticed that I refer to it quite often. I detest walking into it. Anyway, Carrock Fell was not part of this walk and I won't mention it again.

We were invited to sign the visitor's book in the pub and we read of a few other people who had passed this way en route between Lands End and John O'Groats but all the others were cyclists. Not many people walking would come this way but that's their loss. We received a couple more donations and the Art Group had donated £21.15 making a total of £136.15 from the village. Excellent!

PRATS!

Friday, 17 November, Day Twenty-seven, 24 miles
Gretna to Glencapel, all by road

We've been amazed at people's kindness and generosity on our walk and how people have put themselves out to accommodate us, and our needs on our journey. We have tried our very best not to put on people any more than we can help, but today I did something really stupid and caused one of our dearest friends hassle that he could have well done without. Frank brought us coffee in bed for the second day running, we had breakfast and we set off with him in his car towards Gretna where we finished last night. He was dropping us off, prior to travelling to Leeds for an appointment.

We'd travelled about eight miles and Ken turned round to me. "Have you got the camera?" he inquired. I had been responsible for the camera for the whole journey and I had left it in the kitchen at Frank and Rachel's house.

Poor Frank had to go back all the way to Hesket, then to Gretna by which time he was half an hour behind schedule when meant he was letting other people down, and it was my entire fault. I was so cross. We started walking at nine o'clock instead of half past eight but all we could think about was Frank and how we had let him down.

We marched on to Annan, trying to make up for lost time and trying to punish ourselves for our stupidity. We found a butcher's shop and thought we'd buy a pork pie to cheer ourselves up. The butcher's shop had only got Scottish pies so we bought two of those. They weren't as good as pork pies. By the time we stopped to eat them we had walked ten miles.

We stopped by a very beautiful cycle path sign on one of the many cycle paths that have been created as a millennium projects. It was next to Brow Well where Robert Burns had apparently also had a buttie stop at some time when he was travelling this way. He had drunk from the well; we erred on the side of caution and had a drink from our orange juice bottles. Our two small bottles are really well travelled. They are just the throw away sort with a top you can suck from. We bought them in Cornwall and we have just had them refilled each day. They're less than half a litre each but we find it is ample for us; in fact, we have to keep reminding ourselves to take a drink occasionally to avoid the risk of getting dehydrated.

The weather was beautiful so we soon cheered up. We had splendid views of the Solway Firth almost all day and it took our minds back to when we last saw the sea in Cornwall. It seems ironic that, then we were walking almost due east and now, we are walking due west. We're walking 24 miles today we will finish only about three miles further north than when we started. When you look at a map of Great Britain you realise that it has quite a tilt to the west. Edinburgh on the east coast of Scotland is actually further west than Liverpool on the west coast of England.

We made a bit of a mistake with the way we handled the walk today. Walking 24 miles with all our clobber is a lot harder than just walking with a day bag. We really need to have more stops and we only stopped twice today. We were on tarmac all day and it was dry tarmac and my feet got hot and slightly painful again.

We have only got to carry our clobber for three more days and two of those will be quite short ones but we have made our mind up that we must stop three times, not twice during the day. My right foot got quite painful at one stage. I think it's because, when I'm carrying my bag, I am heavier and I land harder on my feet. Walking when something hurts is not a very efficient way of walking.

Lynne and husband Chris Jackson are our hosts tonight and when we arrived at their house there was no one at home. Lynne had walked down the road to look for us coming the scenic route. We had taken the more direct route but Lynne arrived home minutes after we arrived and made us a very welcome coffee, put a packet of Radox in my hand and sent me off for a bath. Was she trying to tell me something?

Their home is only a couple of years old and Chris, who is a builder, built it himself. Chris is a local, and works in partnership with his brother who only lives a couple of miles away. When chatting to him later we discovered that he actually did the building work on the walls that surrounded the Robert Burns Well where we had stopped earlier that day.

Lynne and I have known each other for quite a few years but we lost touch for some time and met up by accident in Dumfries three years ago. They had decided that as this is our first night in Scotland, haggis is the order of the day, which they served in true Scottish style with 'neeps and tatties'. They had invited a few friends and neighbours round to meet us later which was lovely but I was so tired and, despite the fact they were excellent company, I found myself unable to stay awake and had to leave Ken to do the talking and retire early.

It was only the second or third time I'd really felt tired on the whole walk and I think it was a combination of a few late nights, walking too hard with too few stops, walking on dry tarmac and being wound up about the inconvenience I'd caused Frank this morning over the camera incident.

A Day With Megan

Saturday, 18 November, Day Twenty-eight, 24 miles
Glencapel to just past Carron Bridge on major and minor roads

Chris made us porridge for breakfast; Lynne not only made our packed lunch but also is going to carry it for us all day. I protest but she insists, I concur. What is even better is that Chris is going to pick her up at the end of the day which means that we don't have to carry all our clobber and he even agrees to pick us up and deliver us to our hosts for tonight. Does he know what he's letting himself in for? I did gently hint that they live up a mountain vaguely to the north west of Dumfries but not really near anywhere.

We're off for just after eight o'clock, the four of us, that's me and Ken and Lynne with her lovely collie dog Megan. It's a slightly drizzly morning, which is a bit of a shame, because I would have loved to see Glencapel in the sunshine. It's such a pretty place, nestling on the mouth of the River Nith where it meets the Solway Firth.

We follow the Nith on a minor road and are guided by Lynne through Kingholm Quay or Dumfries Docks, and into Dumfries on a cycle track and another Millennium cycle track sign. We make our way through Dumfries, stopping to buy bananas at the market. Bananas, like pork pies, have become a 'must' for us. We have 'three o'clock banana time' and that seems to give us an energy boost that we need to see us through to the end of the day.

We followed the A76 for the rest of the morning. It's not the nicest road to walk along and conversation is constantly interrupted by heavy traffic. We got off the main road on to a very minor road and it was sheer heaven. We stopped to eat our lunch in a forestry plantation near Closeburn and accidentally stumbled across a hole with several dozen whisky bottles buried in it. Now we know we really are in Scotland! We continued on towards Thornhill. The drizzle stopped, the sun came out and the views over the Lowther Hills where we will walk tomorrow were stunning.

We made excellent time and Lynne rang Chris from the phone box at Carron Bridge, which should have been our destination tonight. She told him that we would continue on towards the Dalveen Pass, which would take us up into the Lower Hills, until he was able to pick us up. That was great for us because it would take a couple of uphill miles off tomorrow's walk when we would be carrying our clobber. Chris arrived and drove us to the home of tonight's hosts, friends and former neighbours from Ravenstonedale, Linda and Maurice.

"Sorry we keep our friends in such funny places," we said apologetically as, half an hour of back lanes later, we started on the final approach

Kingholme Quay, Dumfries

Dalveen Pass

up the dead end track that leads to their home. They live in a typical Scottish crofter's cottage. There is one bedroom downstairs, which Linda's mum is using, and two further bedrooms up in the roof space up a narrow central staircase, one of which is ready for us. On the landing is a wonderful little table, the top made from a single slice from the trunk of an oak tree with the central leg made from a twisted trunk of a cherry tree. Maurice is a stone waller, but working is difficult when the weather is inclement so he is hoping to start manufacturing similar pieces to sell. If they are all as attractive as this one he should do well.

We introduced our last night's hosts to our tonight's hosts and then said our farewells to Lynne and Chris and off they went, Lynne being desperate to wallow in a bath tub and also to attend to Megan who had curled up in the back of the car between rucksacks and buckets. Megan is about eleven-years-old and I have known her most of her life. She is more used to being on a lead and being in traffic that Ranger but even she found it hard walking on the main roads. Linda and Maurice have three dogs that greet us with varying degrees of enthusiasm. One is deaf, one is fat and the other is ... well...sixteen. The deaf one has recently taken a dislike to the old one and growls every time it gets to close. The fat one just lies around, not really caring about anything as long as no one pinches its grub.

Linda's mother lives in the Lake District and is staying for a few days. She is 88-years-old, or should we say, young. She has a wonderful mind and wants to know all our adventures. She saw us on the telly the day before we started so knows quite a bit about the walk anyway. Again we have a lovely meal, meat pie and home-grown vegetables. We're chased away from the table to sit by the fire for coffee. Linda's mother insists that the clearing and washing up are her job. Another lovely evening with lovely company. Aren't we lucky to have so many good friends?

RUNNING OUT OF FRIENDS
Sunday, 19 November, Day Twenty-nine, 22 miles
Just past Carron Bridge to Roberton on minor roads and farm tracks, and a mile on Death Alley

Tonight is the first time we're going to have to pay for a bed. We just don't know anyone in the area. Linda and Maurice drive us back to our finishing point last night and off we go, up the Dalveen Pass. There is a bit of a drizzle and now that we are further north and the season is getting later the temperature has dropped quite a bit. We pass a small settlement and a few houses and the drizzle turns to rain but doesn't last for more than a few minutes. It then clears up and the sun comes out and stays fine for the rest of the day.

The scenery is magnificent and the bit of rain had sharpened the views and it was looking its very best for us. We had driven through the Dalveen Pass earlier on this year when we had come to Scotland in the camper van for a few days to reci some of our route. We had thought then that it was stunning, but taking a few hours walking through was entirely different to driving through it. It takes longer to see what delight there is to feast your eyes on around each corner and it never disappoints.

There was hardly any traffic so we were able to enjoy the views in silence. This pass must be one of Scotland's best-kept secrets. The road climbs very slowly and is built almost like a railway line with no undulations and, at its summit at an altitude of about 300m, is the boundary of Dumfries and Galloway.

We were dawdling along, stopping to take photographs when a vehicle passed us slowly and stopped. It was our friend Pete Denby. I think he's determined to get into every chapter of our book. Being Sunday, his shop in Kirkby Stephen is closed and he had decided to take a drive out to see how we were getting on. We stopped for a chat and then he drove further up the pass so that he could find somewhere to park and then film us on his video camera as we walked. We met up with him again later when we stopped for our lunch. By then we were walking down the pass.

We crossed over the Southern Upland Way, which follows the road for a short time and continued on through Elvanfoot and joined the A702, which took us under the M74 to Crawford where there is a real transport cafe. It was about half past two and we stopped for an 'all day breakfast' which was our main meal today as the place we are staying tonight doesn't do evening meals. The people at the B&B are away for the weekend and we don't want to get there too early but we linger longer than we should.

WHEN THE JUGGERNAUTS PASSED US
WE HAD TO STOP AND ALMOST CLAMBER
INTO THE HEDGE .....

"It would be quicker on the M74"

We set off on our way again. We are following the A702, which clings to the side of the motorway and is very noisy, but we look hard at the map and there are a series of farm tracks, between the railway line and the River Clyde, and it will add no distance to our walk, so we take that route. There is a bit of a problem in that it is starting to get dark, but the tracks are tarmac or gravel all the way so we don't have too much trouble. We can see and hear the M74 and the A702 in the distance. They are both very busy and very noisy but too far away to cause us any hassle. The track crosses the infant River Clyde and joins the A702 just after the turn off for Roberton where we are staying tonight and, as we look into the distance, all the traffic seems to be heading on the minor road through Roberton instead of the main road, and we can't understand why.

We scramble up a bank on to the A702 and it is deserted. We walk a few yards in the darkness and find a 'road closed' sign. We go through a little lane on to the Roberton road. It is a single carriageway each way with no footpath and there are continuous lines of traffic speeding each way, including juggernauts heading for the M74.

We attach our fluorescent strips to our jacket sleeves and walk the last mile into Roberton. I was terrified. I couldn't see because of the blinding lights and when the juggernauts passed us we had to stop and almost clamber into the hedge to stop ourselves being dragged along by them.

There were newly laid kerb stones but nothing behind them so when we leapt off the road to make room for the largest of the vehicles to pass us we had no idea what we were standing on. It was very frightening and very dangerous. Again I am thankful not to have Ranger with us. We eventually got to the B&B and were served coffee and biscuits before retiring to our nice room for a hot bath and an early night.

WE'VE MADE A NEW FRIEND!
Monday, 20 November, Day Thirty, 20 miles
Roberton to Forth almost all on very minor roads

We'd already told our hosts that we didn't eat cooked breakfast but would like a couple of cheese sandwiches for our packed lunch. Breakfast was beautifully served with oat cakes and Scotch pancakes as well as toast and cereals. When we came to settle the bill Mrs. Craig said she would only charge £16 for one of us and would donate the charge for the other one to our fund.

I couldn't believe it. I thought that they might give us a donation but I really didn't expect generosity like this. They were a semi-retired couple and I'm sure they got more pleasure out of giving the money to the charity than they would have got out of spending it. We accepted the donation and promised to send them a copy of our finishing 'round robin' letter.

We set off in glorious sunshine and for the first time we are crunching ice under our boots. We were on the A73 for the first six miles and stopped for a break in a graveyard at St John's Kirk where the A73 and A72 meet. At first glance it appeared to have only old tombstones, but then I spotted six identical small modern headstones. They were the graves of six Polish Forces men, all of whom had died in the latter part of 1940. I imagine that they must have originally been simple markers on the graves and have been recently been replaced, possibly to commemorate the 50th anniversary of the end of the war. I looked around the other tombstones for interesting inscriptions but found none as interesting as one I had been recently told of.

A friend called Mary who lives in Shropshire had parents whose marriage was far from harmonious. She was very fond of her mother but had little time for her father. The marriage survived, but in name only, right through to the 'till death do us part' bit and her father piously had a stone erected on his wife's grave which read:

'The time has passed, but not the pain,
We shall not see her likes again'

When her father died a few years later it fell to Mary to think of something suitable to add to the tombstone in his memory.

"I don't know how I got away with it, obviously someone wasn't paying attention when they rubber-stamped the approval," she told me. It read:

'The time has passed, we all concur,
The pain himself lies here with her'.

I don't think I would have believed the story but she took out a photograph of it. Believe me, it's true. We continued on in glorious sunshine though Thankerton and stripped down to T-shirts and stopped again for lunch just before we crossed the Clyde for the last time. It's been with us for a couple of days now, getting bigger all the time.

Next we crossed the railway line at Carstairs Junction where the Edinburgh, Glasgow and London railway lines all meet. Just after that we passed a very large compound with security fencing. It is marked on the map as a hospital but it is obvious that they have a few people in there that they don't want to let out. We crossed over the A70 and back onto another minor road to Braehead, heading for Forth (or The Forth as those in the know call it). This is the top of the watershed, and we cross on to the east coast watershed for the very first time.

I know everyone reading this will know what I mean by 'watershed' but I was quite surprised, when guiding a walk recently, that no one in the group knew what I was talking about when I said that we'd stop for lunch when we'd crossed the watershed. They all thought I was going to produce a portable telly and make them wait until after nine o'clock and tune it into something rude. The word 'watershed' seems to have taken a new meaning.

As we were heading towards Wilsontown, a car pulled up and a lady called us over so that she could put some money in our bucket. As we were thanking her we saw two people approaching us. They were our hosts for the next three nights Alan and Beryl Naylor who we have known for many years through the Ski Club, and shared a holiday with a couple of years ago. They had seen us in the distance and Alan had been filming us with his video camera, which has a very powerful zoom lens. They accused us of trying to hitch a lift! We pointed out that the car was actually going in the wrong direction anyway.

We walked back with them to their car, which they had left at our finishing point for tonight and drove us back over tomorrow's route. Tomorrow we will finish back at their home. Beryl retired from work a couple of weeks ago and is feeling very pleased with herself and looking very fit and radiant. She and Alan have a lovely spacious bungalow and Beryl produces a delicious meal.

THIS OTHER AVON
Tuesday, 21 November, Day Thirty-one, 16 miles
Forth to Candie with Alan and Beryl showing us the lovely footpaths through the Avon Gorge

We have a short day today so dawdle over breakfast. Alan delivered us back to the spot where we finished last night and returned back to home, as he and Beryl are going to walk from home, back to meet us and be our guides this afternoon. Again we are crunching ice, in glorious sunshine, with barely a breath of wind. We set off running, as we aren't carrying our clobber. Ken has our jackets attached to the top of his rucksack and they remain there all day. I carry nothing at all.

We reach Longridge, and a fairly old lady is walking along the road in front of us with her dog. She has a plastic bag covering her hand and keeps stopping to pick up litter and pops it in the plentiful litter bins all along the main street. I stop to talk to her, to congratulate her and to tell her she deserves a medal for her actions and we both share our opinions on people who drop litter.

As we have run and walked along hundreds of miles of grass verges during our walk, we've been appaled at the amount of litter - bottles, cans, wrappers, etc. - we even found a mobile phone a couple of days ago. The problem is, that if we are running along a grass verge it would be very easy to step on a bottle or can and cause an accident. We are feeling that, physically and mentally, nothing can stop us achieving our goal of arriving at John O'Groats on 3 December, but something as simple as breaking an ankle on a discarded can or bottle could ruin everything. We

Avon Bridge, Falkirk

are enjoying every minute of our adventure and don't want it to end but we also know that we're not there yet and a lot of things could still go wrong.

We spend the morning running along the A706 but the traffic is very light and no problem at all and we arrive in Whitburn far earlier than we expect to, so ring Alan and Beryl to suggest they get on their way, otherwise we'll be back at Candie before they leave!

We continue on and find a bacon buttie wagon. We stop to buy one and the young chap only charges us £1 and the other £2 goes in our box. We think it's a lovely gesture; he's only a young lad and obviously works hard for a living. We walk on through Armadale and meet Alan and Beryl and we're soon off the road and on to a lovely footpath along the Avon Gorge. It is a real delight, aglow with autumn colours enhanced by the magnificent afternoon sunshine.

We cross over the river on a little wooden bridge and my mind goes back to when we crossed the other River Avon, on the cycle track attached to the M5 with a howling gale pushing us along. We keep stopping feast our eyes, and also our stomachs and Ken takes a photograph of me, in sheer heaven, eating my 'three o'clock banana' sitting on a fallen branch in the glorious sunshine.

Dovecotes near the Firth

We climbed out of the gorge and Alan and Beryl guide us back to their home across fields. It was lovely to have walkers with local knowledge to guide us because Scotland has different rules on rights of way and the route they took us wasn't shown on our map. We all head back to Candie together; Beryl serves us another lovely meal and we enjoy another evening in excellent company. We may not be millionaires but we have untold wealth in friends.

OVER THE FIRTH OF FORTH

Wednesday, 22 November, Day Thirty-two, 24 miles

Candie to just past Yetts O'Muckhart, too much on major roads

K en and I get up early to try to get away without disturbing Alan and Beryl. It's a big advantage walking back to the place where we're sleeping in so that we don't have to rely on anyone giving us a lift and we can make a better start. We're on our way before eight o'clock. It's raining, not heavily but we've had so little rain on the whole walk we've almost forgotten what rain is. It soon stops but there is still a bit off drizzle every now and again. We head towards Falkirk on a B road. We've not been going too long when Ken points out a vast expanse of sea in the distance. I suppose you could argue that it's really the Firth of Forth but to us it is our first glance of the sea on the east coast so it's quite a landmark.

We find ourselves in a council estate, then a building site and then an industrial estate. We crossed over the Union canal and stopped to look at it. Five miles further west there is major project in progress to re-connect it to the Forth and Clyde Canal. There was originally a flight of locks but our clever engineers have come up with something unique, Falkirk Wheel which will transfer boats from one to another by lifting them or dropping them eighty feet, floating in a tank of water. It sounds incredible. It is due to open soon and should be quite a spectacle and well worth a visit.

We go under the M9, cross the River Carron and then manage to get off the main road at last and stop for a short break. We're just on our way again and Alan draws up in the car and kicks Beryl out to walk with us for the next ten miles. It's quite pleasant on the back roads but all good things must come to an end and we join the A876 to cross over the River Forth on the Kincardine Bridge. Like all the large river crossings, it is hell and I emerge at the far end behaving like a gibbering wreck. We are now in the Kingdom of Fyfe, and come straight off the main road down some steps into Kincardine village, which is really nice. We manage to keep off the main road for another mile by walking through the grounds of the Police Training Collage where we found some suitable flat stones and sat down for our lunch, then it's back on another main road, this time it's the A977.

We look into the distance and see the lovely Ochil Hills and after a couple of days of flat and industrial landscape we are ready for a change. Alan reappears so that he can walk with us and Beryl departs for home. She is going to pick us up at the end of the day. We continue on, through Dollar, which is a lovely village, and a couple of people put donations in our bucket. The walk from Dollar to Yetts O'Muckhart was far from enjoyable. It was raining most of the time but that wasn't the problem, the problem was the traffic. Not that it was heavy but it seemed to be constant and I felt it was quite a strain.

We finally got to the turning for the B934, which takes us through the mountains to Dunning. Although it is starting to get dark we continue to walk for a further two and a half miles until Beryl arrives to pick us up.

We returned to Candie for a third night and took Alan and Beryl out to the pub for a meal and return for our last night in a bed we are now quite familiar with. Apart from our four days in our own bed in the middle bit, it is the first time we've had more than two nights in the same bed.

Peter is on his way north tonight with Ranger and they are meeting us first thing in the morning to take us back to our today's finishing point. Tomorrow night we will be back to being gypsies. We are already beginning to feel like people of the road, having walked more than 700 miles so far but we still keep reminding ourselves, 'we ain't there till we get there'.

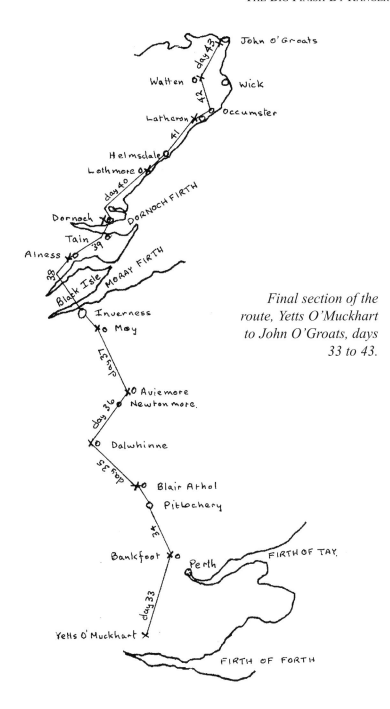

Final section of the route, Yetts O'Muckhart to John O'Groats, days 33 to 43.

I'M HERE AGAIN - BY RANGER

Thursday, 23 November, Day Thirty-three, 25 miles

Just past Yetts O'Muckhart to Bankfoot, mostly on very minor roads and footpaths

Peter drove me up last night and we slept in the van. We met up with the 2Ks at half past eight and took them to where they reckon they finished last night. It seemed a long way, to me. I hope they're not cheating. On the way they stop at the lovely village of Dollar to buy a few groceries. Kathy tries to buy a haggis but there isn't a butchers and the supermarket doesn't have any. She buys 'nips and 'tatties and tells Peter to go in search of a haggis while we're out walking. Seems they've not forgotten how to boss Peter around.

It's ten o'clock before we actually start and the sun is shining and all is well. We are all so happy to be back together again. We set off up the lovely road to Dunning and hardly see any traffic. We have been walking for an hour or so when a car approaches and slows down. It is a friend of the 2Ks called John Knight who lives in Leamington Spar and has decided to combine visiting relatives in Scotland with a day or two walking with the 2Ks. He has been checking our progress on our web site that Libby keeps updating. Clever what?

John is no stranger to long distance walking. Three years ago he walked the Appalachian Way in America, which is more than twice the distance of our adventure. John spends a couple of hours with us and then returns to his car to go and find a B&B and we hope to meet up with him later.

We meet Peter and have butties in the van, just like the good old days down south. Peter has managed to acquire a haggis free of charge. He inquired at the Post Office in Dunning where he could get a haggis and was directed a mile or so down the road to a haggis farm where the boss of the company was alerted to his need and he had found a brave haggis on the farm who willing to give up it's life for the benefit of our heroes! We leave the van in a mess for Peter to clean up and off we go again.

For the first time we actually walk a little way along the A9, the new enemy. It's sort of the Scottish equivalent to the A30 we hated so much in the south and we will be following it for about 200 miles. Actually, it's not too bad but in our eagerness to get off of it, we take a short cut along a track, that ends up in a sort of dump. The problem is that, in Scotland the rules on rights of way are different from in England and therefore a path on the map is just a path, which may or may not be a right of way and might just go to nowhere.

We end up wrestling our way through a jungle alongside a raging torrent, which is between us and the road we would like to be on. The options are lifting me over the fence into someone's garden and past their lounge window and up their drive, or a bit more jungle and wrestling a tiger. They choose the tiger and won. They just get back on the road when someone stops them and asks if he can photograph them for the *Dundee News*. You should have seen the state of them, still bearing the scars from tiger wrestling. Just look like a pair of tramps.

We continue on and it's a bit further than we thought and we end up finishing in the dark. Peter and John are both waiting for us and we find a funky Cyber Cafe with funky food. Not what you'd expect in the wilds of Scotland but we all enjoy a meal together. John departs to his B&B and we go and look for somewhere to camp. We drive back along the road but can't find a suitable lay-by, so return to Bankfoot to the Tourist Information Centre car park, which has a nice handy grass verge for Peter's tent.

With John Knight at Bankford

We're just nicely settled in and put the kettle on for a cuppa when a car pulls up with blue flashing lights. Peter invites Mr. Plod to join us, but he declines. He's looking for people breaking into houses, so he says. We wonder if his vigilance has something to do with the whisky distillery, which is next door. Peter tells him what we're doing and Mr. Plod almost apologises to us for not being able to offer more suitable accommodation. We wonder if he is going to offer us a nice warm cell but he just wishes us well and drives off and we all turn in for the night, me on my candlewick bedspread, that pair on their spring interior mattress under their down duvet and poor Peter in his tent.

I DO MY RADIO BIT
Friday, 24 November, Day Thirty-four, 25 miles
Bankfoot to Blair Athol on footpaths and the Glasgow to Inverness Cycle Track

It's another sunny day but there's low lying mist so it's quite cold but we run to keep warm. They spotted a track on the map that is straighter than the road and we manage to navigate it without any mishaps. A gamekeeper accosts us just before we rejoin the road. He tells us that they are about to start a shoot. Poor grouse, it doesn't take a lot of skill to shoot them as they aren't very good at flying but if people would rather pay a fortune to kill their own instead of buying their meat at the butchers like the rest of us, should we complain? It's instant death and it keeps a bit of money flowing from the very rich to the very poor.

We cross the River Tay at Dunkeld, where we meet John who has driven back to Bankfoot and missed us because we took the track instead of the road. John tells us that he is going to drive on a few miles and walk back to meet us. A few miles further on we join the Inverness to Glasgow Cycle Route at Logierait which we will be following all the way to Inverness, give or take a little diversion or two. The walking is lovely. Mostly we can't hear or see the A9 and we're beginning to think of it as more like a guiding light than an enemy. We meet John just before lunch, by which time we've walked about sixteen miles. We eat lunch in the van and John walks about half a mile with us before departing to visit his son. It's been lovely to spend a bit of time with him.

Peter meets us again in Pitlochry. We have decided to do a bit extra and go on to Blair Athol, another seven miles. We're walking along the road minding our own business when a car pulls up with three men in and asks for directions to the Youth Hostel. We point it out on our map and then they ask about our walk and congratulate us on our achievement so far. As they pull away they notice our bucket and call us back. "Didn't realise you were collecting for charity," they said, dropping £10 into it. And they dare to accuse the Scots of being mean!

We get there about half past four, just before dark and Peter drives us back to Pitlochry to a B&B that one of our blind friends, Ivan Pickford has put us in touch with. We find it with no difficulty and the 2Ks are busy trying to get their boots off to make themselves look more respectable before they get out of the van when Andrew Brown, the proprietor, comes out and introduces himself and tells us that we're booked into the local radio station for an interview at half past five.

They have a quick bath and all pile into the van. It's only five minutes to the radio studio and they want to interview the whole team, including me. We're all taken into the padded cell. I didn't actually say anything but they did tell the listeners what a star I am and the presenter gave us £5; live on air, for our funds. We then celebrated our stardom with a slap up meal, me in the van and them at the chippy, before retiring to bed, me in the van and them in nice bedrooms at Mr. Brown's B&B.

INTO THE HIGHLANDS

Saturday, 25 November, Day Thirty-five, 25 miles

Blair Athol to Dalwhinnie, mostly on the Cycle Track

Peter comes to my boudoir to feed me breakfast, the other lazy pair are probably still asleep or arguing about socks. The wet and dirty ones were left in the van last night and created an aroma for which I will no doubt get the blame. Mr. Brown serves them a lovely breakfast and when they come to pay the bill he tells them there is no charge. Mr. Brown did the same thing for two years for our blind friends. Hospitality goes round and round. We tell Mr. Brown he is welcome to stay with us any time he is travelling south, thank him and were on our way and back tramping the road again by a quarter to nine. We drive back to Blair Athol where we finished walking last night.

Blair Athol is unique in that it is the only place in Britain to have its own private army. Queen Victoria gave permission to the Duke to have a private army, which consists of about thirty soldiers who are actually mostly estate workers. It parades once a year sometime in May. The present Duke, who actually lives in South Africa, comes to the castle to review it.

It's rained most of the night so the 2Ks have their jackets on to start with, but the sun soon comes out. We follow the River Garry all morning and meet up with Peter for lunch and then continue up Glen Garry to Drumochter Pass. At an altitude of 426 meters it is the highest trunk road in Britain and the greatest altitude we will reach in Scotland. At the top of the pass we cross into the Highlands of Scotland.

The cycle path is a delight to walk on. Mostly we are away from the main road and on the short stretches that are along side the road there is a barrier and we feel very safe. We see a plaque on the side of one of the many little bridges that take the cycle track over the side streams. It marks the spot where a cyclist was killed in August 1999 cycling from Lands End to John O'Groats. We give a little thought to the poor chap. By this stage he would probably have been only two or three days from

his destination. It's a very sobering thought and reminds us that 'we ain't there till we get there'. We notice that all the foot-bridges have very large stones at each end of them that are painted white and wonder if that is because the man failed to see the bridge and skidded off into the stream.

We continue on and they have their 'three o'clock banana', which has become a bit of a ritual. In the distance they see a bright green jacket coming towards

them. It's Peter who has parked the van at Dalwhinnie, our destination for tonight, and walked four miles back to meet us. They share their half past three chocolate with him as they walk and then it starts to rain. We were two and a half miles from our destination and you can get very wet in two and a half miles.

The 2Ks blame Peter. This is the wettest they've been since Taunton. We arrive at Dalwhinnie a very soggy mess and camping doesn't seem so appealing. The 2Ks book a room at the Travel Lodge, £35 room only and you only get one and a half towels but they all have a bath and dry their clobber.

We're veritably unimpressed with Dalwhinnie. Everything about it has a 'closed for the season' feel about it. Even the famous distillery is closed. They suspect that the food in the restaurant won't be too exciting so Kathy returned to the van to cook the haggis, 'neeps and 'tatties they had acquired three days ago. A good meal is enjoyed and then they return to the over priced room with the dirty dishes in a carrier bag to do the washing up, have coffee and watch the telly. Peter comes back to the van just after nine o'clock and we sleep together again. People will be talking!

Really Enjoying Myself

Sunday, 26 November, Day Thirty-six, 25 miles

Dalwhinnie to Aviemore, half on the Cycle Track, half on minor roads.

The 2Ks appear bright and early for breakfast in the van and we're off by a quarter to eight. It rained most of the night but stops just as we set off. Apart from a wee bit of drizzle it is fine all day. We're following the River Turim to start with, and that joins the Spey, which we follow for the rest of the day. It has warmed up considerable and they soon take off their jackets and they don't go back on again all day, quite remarkable for the Highlands at the end of November.

The sun manages to put in a sort appearance and makes us another rainbow so obviously someone has had some rain but we manage to miss it as usual. The low cloud lifts later and we can see the Cairngorms covered in snow, but the warm weather has make the snow very patchy on the lower slopes. We meet up with Peter at Kingussie for lunch. Kingussie should have been our destination for tonight but we are going on a further twelve miles to Aviemore.

Our mate Pete Denby has paid for a night at a B&B for us tonight at Newtonmoor, which we pass through just before Kingussie. Our Peter has been and found the place so we won't have to search for it tonight in the dark. We continue on to Aviemore and arrive at about four o'clock.

We're fine, but Kathy complains about being tired. She didn't sleep well last night at the Travel Lodge and also wonders if she is eating enough of the right food.

Peter is waiting for us at the railway station as agreed and drives us back to the B&B at Newtonmoor, where the proprietors, Mr. and Mrs. Stewart greeted them with tea and chocolate cake. We're not too sure what the arrangements for Peter are but it seems that some other philanthropic person who was staying at the B&B recently and knew about our walk has paid for Peter to stay at the B&B as well.

I get my dinner and, as I will be sleeping in the van on my own again tonight and intend sleeping on the spring interior mattress with down duvet, they sensibly put my candlewick bedspread on the bed instead of the front passenger seat where I am supposed to sleep.

They all go off to the pub for a meal. Peter and Ken have an excellent venison casserole and Peter asks the landlady if she would like to adopt him. We return to the B&B, by which time Pete Denby has also turned up as he is also staying here tonight. There is good crack helped along with a 'wee dram' and then off to their beds which Mrs Stewart has thoughtfully put hot water bottles in.

KATHY'S POORLY FOOT DAY
Monday, 27 November, Day Thirty-seven, 22 miles
Aviemore to just past Moy on the A9 and on the Cycle Track

They have the first cooked breakfast they've had for the whole walk. They have declined cooked breakfast whenever it was offered because they find walking on a belly full of eggs and bacon a bit hard, but as Pete Denby has paid for their breakfast and is going to eat with them it seems a but naughty not to eat it. It's the full works including porridge and home made oat cakes. Our Peter drove us back to Aviemore and it's nearly nine o'clock before we start walking. Kathy takes longer than normal to walk off the 'morning stiffness'.

After about three miles she realises that the problem is more serious. It feels like a sprained ankle but she can't remember injuring it. She then realises that it is the ankle that she broke skiing about a dozen years ago and has been known to cause a problem in the past. She can walk on it without too much pain but running on it is out, so consequently progress is slower. Most of the morning we are on roads and although they're not major roads there is a bit of traffic so we're not too happy.

We get back onto the cycle track at Carrbridge and it takes us over Slochd summit, an altitude of 406 meters, in glorious sunshine. There can't be many people lucky enough to cross the summit in sunshine, but to do it in this weather at this time of year is incredible. From here we start heading down to sea level for most of the rest of the journey and we really feel that the weather has been so kind to us. Whatever it does from here it won't cause us any problems.

We meet up with Peter for lunch just before Tomatin and then he goes ahead to find somewhere to camp and get his tent up before it gets dark. He meets up with us again at four o'clock to tell us he's pitched his tent three miles ahead. It's getting dark by then so I get in the van and drive ahead with Peter. Actually I was glad to get in the van with Peter as Kathy's language was getting appaling. It seem that she can walk on her ankle but not without swearing. They arrive at five o'clock and cook sausages and mash with onions and peas for their dinner. This is going to be our last night camping and I think we're very lucky to be able to camp comfortably in the north of Scotland this late in the year.

THE GREAT GLEN AND THE BLACK ISLE
Tuesday, 28 November, Day Thirty-eight, 28 miles
Moy To Alness on the Inverness by-pass, some lovely lanes and footpaths and a couple of Firths

We're off before 7.30am and it's not even daylight. That's one of the big advantages of camping: we usually manage to get an early start. Kathy's foot seems to have made a full recovery and camping could also have helped in that. It is impossible to stand up in the camper van so Kathy has not put any weight on her foot for over fourteen hours, except for one very quick nip outside. Anyway Kathy is now a happier person and didn't say 'bugger' once today. I won't tell you how many times she said it yesterday.

We meet up with Peter after three miles because then they have to walk for six miles on the A9 on the outskirts of Inverness. Then they have to negotiate the Kessock Bridge over the Beauly Firth and they don't think I'll enjoy it much. The Beauly Firth is where the Great Glen meets the sea and is connected to Loch Ness by the Caledonian Canal at Inverness. We meet up with the 2Ks and I walk over the Black Isle with them. When me and the 2Ks were up here in the spring, we discovered a wonderful butcher at Fortrose who made award-winning haggis so Peter is sent off to find the shop and buy more haggis, or is it haggi?

We manage to walk right across the Black Isle without seeing the A9 once. We meet up with Peter again just before the minor road joins the A9 to cross over the Cromarty Firth and off the Black Isle. They decide that walking over the bridge won't be a lot of fun for me. Like the Kessock Bridge, it's over a mile long including the approaches and although it has a good footpath it's not nice to walk over. When we meet them again the light is starting to fade and they decide to leave me in the van for the rest of the day. It's just as well because the road into Alness is very busy.

It seems further than they thought it was. Why is the last mile always the longest? By the time they get there it is dark and they are wearing their reflective strips on their jackets, having been ticked off by a policeman for causing a traffic hazard. We're all tired but very happy to have had a successful day. The weather has been perfect: not a drop of rain.

Kathy's ankle has made a full recovery. Yesterday she had thought for the first time since we left Lands End that she might not make it to John O'Groats. Although we still know that 'we ain't there till we get there' we're feeling so fit and good and we're pretty confident that all will be well, barring accidents of course. As they are getting into the van at Alness, they spot an Indian take away cum chippy. They have told Cynthia, our host for the next three nights, not to prepare anything for them tonight so they get take aways and eat them in the van. What a pong, lamb tikka, steak pie, fish and chips and boots that have walked 850 miles, and I bet they try to blame the smells in the van on me.

We drive the 20 miles on to Dornoch where we will walk to tomorrow. Cynthia Swallow is a former walking holiday guest. Her husband John is in hospital at the moment having his knee joint replaced so, sadly we won't get to see him. Their house has, in the past been two houses and there is quite a lot of it and we are accommodated in the cottage bit with our own bathroom. Cynthia loves dogs so I am made very welcome. She has a lovely springer spaniel called Tilly, and I disgrace myself, first by nicking her bed and then trying to pick a fight with her because she won't let me play with her ball. Cynthia gives the boys a whisky and Kathy a sherry which I knock flying with my tail. I'm not used to coffee tables. I really am letting them down but Cynthia is quite unperturbed and just pours Kathy another glass of sherry.

Ken rings logistics. It seems that it's now Ravenstonedale's turn to get rained on and the village school has water lapping around the door for the first time in living memory. We haven't seen a drop of rain for three days.

THE FINAL FORTH

Wednesday, 29 November, Day Thirty-nine, 20 miles
Alness to Dornoch, mostly on minor roads

We drive back to Alness and we're walking by about half past eight, along a lovely minor road which runs parallel to the A9 but about three or four miles to the north of it. It's a delight, hardly any traffic, wandering in and out of luscious woodland and there are occasional stunning views of the Cromarty Firth that we crossed yesterday. We meet up with Peter for lunch after about twelve miles. He has managed to acquire more pork pies. What a star that man is.

Immediately after lunch we meet up with our old friend the A9, which we follow for about five miles from Tain and over the Dornoch Firth. Kathy intensely dislikes crossing bridges. She always has a Mars bar to help her across and has managed quite well up to now but this, the last one, one of the shortest and least busy traffic wise, somehow scares her. She starts running. It's over a mile long and she doesn't stop until she can't see any water at the side, by which time she's exhausted. Silly woman. Anyway, it makes for good time.

We come off the A9 just after the bridge, climb over a fence and we're on a very minor road for the last five miles into Dornoch. We arrive back at Cynthia's house by three o'clock to find a freshly baked cake waiting to be eaten. Cynthia does quite a bit of baking for church fund raising things and for a few of the old people in Dornoch. She's only 84 and is the sort of person you would pay to have at your dinner table.

One of the favourite stories we recall is, when at about six years of age she was taken to a family gathering at the Belsfield Hotel on Windermere. She was really impressed by the whole experience, the gracious waitresses in their black dresses and starched hats and pinnies and

KATHY DISLIKES BRIDGES.
SHE ALWAYS HAS A MARS BAR
TO HELP HER ACROSS....

the stately setting. Her parents weren't rich, she told us, (although I think they couldn't have been too poor), and they didn't have a nanny

When it came to bed-time, she was sent off with a male cousin of about her age who did have a nanny. Cynthia had no brothers, only sisters, and had never seen a boy without clothes. When she saw his 'thing' and then saw him pee out of it she thought 'that's a handy little gadget'. At 84 she relates this and many other similar stories until everyone is in stitches. People like her are such a pleasure to know and it's an honour to call her a friend.

Peter had picked up a supermarket 'Chinese ready meal' which he and Ken managed to warm up in the microwave and they served it in Cynthia's elegant dining room. It was washed down with enough wine and whisky to make anything enjoyable.

Heavenly Views

Thursday, 30 November, Day forty, 23 miles

Dornoch to Lothmore on minor roads and the A9

We spend most of the morning walking along the shores of Loch Fleet in glorious sunshine. Kathy keeps stopping to take photographs and admire the view. We are so lucky to have weather like this. We join the A9 and the traffic isn't too bad, but some of the cars travel very fast and I have to be on my lead for the rest of the day.

We pass a newsagents hoarding in the village of Golspie. The headlines are all about rumours that Madonna is planning to get married at Dornoch Cathedral with a wedding feast at Skelbo Castle, which we passed close to this morning. Dornoch Cathedral is Cynthia's parish church. She used to brew the communion wine for them until quite recently. The people who owned Skelbo Castle before it became a hotel were also friends of hers and she used to help them pick fruit in the grounds and make jam to sell at church sales. "I just used to knock and go in," she told us, "it took the servants such a long time to get to the door so I saved them the walk."

We stop for a short while for the 2Ks to unwrap yet another pork pie.

Pete Denby

A van pulls up and two people get out and ask about our walk. They saw us passing their house on the shore of Lock Fleet earlier this morning. They put a donation in our bucket and I am in luck as well because they are 'doggie people' and the lady just happens to have a few dog biscuits in her pocket, which she gives to me.

We plod on a bit further and pass the lovely Dunrobin Castle, which, unlike Skelbo Castle, is open to the public. It looks a lovely place. We make yet another mental note of somewhere we must return to when we have a less pressing engagement in the far north. We continue on for a few more miles and, our friend Pete Denby passes us. He stops further along the road to video us yet again. He is going home today so we bid him farewell and hope that next time we see him will be on our triumphant return home when we will have finished our walk, we hope.

We meet up with our Peter and then walk on a further three miles. By now it's three o'clock and the light is beginning to fade so I remain in the van and the 2Ks continue on for another four miles. We drive back to Dornoch and Cynthia insists that she is going to cook a meal for us tonight. We will be spending the next two nights with another friend of the 2Ks, Hazel Agnew, who lives near Reiss, Berriedale, which is very convenient for us.

We have asked Cynthia and Tilly, who I have now stopped fighting

123

with, if they would do us the honour of walking the last mile and over the finishing line with us on Sunday and then joining us for a celebration dinner at the Castle Hotel in Dornoch. (I don't suppose Tilly and me will be included mind.) They have also asked Cynthia if it will be all right for us to stay with her again on Sunday and drive back to Cumbria on Monday. Cumbria, home, it seems like another world! Cynthia cooks them a lovely dinner and puddings included home made treacle tart, raspberries and cream and home made meringues, which Kathy loves but, try as she might, is unable to eat them all.

UPS AND DOWNS
Friday, 1 December, Day forty-one, 25 miles
Lothmore to Latheron, all on the A9

We arrange with Cynthia for Peter to pick her up on Sunday morning to join us for the big finish, and leave Dornoch to drive to last night's finishing point. We're on the road before half past eight. It's a beautiful day and for most of it we have breathtaking sea views. The road does amazing things, climbing fearlessly in and out of the glens and then descending into deep valleys and climbing out again.

Helmsdale

124

At Portgower, a man who seemed to have some sort of speech problem, stops us to put a donation in our bucket. Just a pound or so but I suspect it was quite a lot of money to him. I never cease to be amazed at people's generosity. I am also embarrassed that I had initially tried to ignore him because I thought he was drunk.

We descend into Helmsdale, which has a pretty little harbour, get down almost to sea level and then up we go again to about 150 meters. It might not sound a lot but it's quite a climb from sea level. We do the same again at Berridale and see the van parked half way up the next ascent. Although we're on the A9 all day the traffic isn't a big problem. There are a few big vehicles, many of them carrying logs, Christmas trees or cattle, and a few buses, but they drive quite cautiously. Some of the cars are a bit of a problem because they travel a bit too fast. The sun shines for most of the day and the only complaint is that it's too hot! Peter meets us again about a mile before our final destination and, like yesterday, I am put in the van as the light is fading.

We drive to meet them at the end. It's not quite four o'clock when they appear and it starts to rain but they're in the van before they get wet. So far they've walked over nine hundred miles and it's only seriously rained

Cynthia's elegant diding room

on them for about ten miles. Somebody must be saying a prayer for them. I wonder if it's that postman in Cornwall?

Hazel, who we are staying with tonight, won't be home until about half past eight, so we drive towards her home, following the route we will take tomorrow. Most of it is on a very straight minor road. It looks exceedingly boring but at least I will be able to be off my lead.

We park up in a picnic spot and I get my dinner. They have decided that they will cook one of the haggi that Peter bought on the Black Isle a few days ago. They still have half a turnip and a few spuds left. Now this haggis was the real thing and came in a sheep's stomach jacket, whereas the one Peter had acquired at Dunning a couple of weeks ago was wearing a plastic raincoat. Dinner was served, dishes were washed and we then proceeded to Hazel's house for coffee, donuts, baths and bed.

THE LONG STRAIGHT ROAD
Saturday, 2 December, Day Forty-Two, 20 miles
Latheron to Watten, mostly on minor roads

Hazel decided to walk with us today. Peter dropped us off at last night's finishing point and we're on our way by half past eight. The sun shines for part of the day and again, there isn't a drop of rain. We continue to follow the main coast road for about four miles and the wind is blowing from the side and is quite cold so they have their jackets on all day.

We turn off the main road onto a minor road and, bliss - I am off my lead again. The minor road is dead straight heading exactly magnetic north and we have the wind behind us for the rest of the day. We meet up with Peter near Camster Cairns and Hazel took them for a guided tour. They are chambered Neolithic burial cairns over 4,500-years-old. I sit in the van with Peter while they crawl inside one of them. It is about 55 feet in diameter and about twelve feet high on the outside.

It's quite difficult to get inside and they have to crawl on their hands and knees for about twenty feet but once they were inside they could stand upright in the chamber, which was about ten feet high and six feet wide. The original top has collapsed but it has been reconstructed using a clear plastic dome to let the daylight in. We continue on our way. The

Camster Cairns

road is long and straight but it's not a long walk today and we seem to finish in no time.

I have disgraced myself once more. This time I found something really interesting to roll in. I think I smell nice, but no one shares my sentiments on the matter. I am taken into Hazel's garage and The Bucket is filled with hot soapy water and I am given a wash before I'm allowed into the house. I still smell a bit, but Kathy says she still loves me. It's nice to know who your real friends are.

There are mixed feelings about tomorrow. We still aren't there but we're pretty confident that it is now 'when' rather than 'if'. We plan to arrive at 2.00pm. Peter is going to drop us off at today's finishing point and then drive to Dornoch to pick up Cynthia and Tilly and book a celebration dinner for the four of them at the Castle Hotel tomorrow. He'll then drive up to John O'Groats and meet us on the main road so that Cynthia can walk over the finishing line with us.

THE BIG FINISH

Sunday, December 3, Day Forty-three, 14 miles
Watten to John O'Groats on minor roads

Peter drops us off at nine o'clock and sets off to pick Cynthia up as planned. It will be a 150 mile round trip for him and we have five hours to walk fourteen miles, so we take our time. The weather is beautiful, the sun shines all day and there is a very light breeze at our back. This road is like the one we were on yesterday, very long, very straight and fairly flat. Each time we come to the top of a rise we hope to see the sea and each time all we see is another rise. I really don't know that we want to see the sea because that will mean that journey's end is in sight and I'm not sure if we're ready for that yet.

Eventually we come to the top of a rise and see it, spread out in front of us with the sun shining on Ducansby lighthouse so brightly it almost looks like a fairground. We join the Thurso to John O'Groats road about four miles west of the junction with the Wick to John O'Groats road, where we thought we were meeting Peter and Cynthia. We check the time and realise that we've dawdled a bit too much and, if we want to be

at the junction by quarter to two as arranged, we'll have to do a bit of jogging.

We're about two miles away when we see someone coming towards us on a bike. It's Hazel. Hazel doesn't have a car and travels everywhere by bike. She shouts words of encouragement. A mile and a half later we were still jogging and we passed Hazel who had stopped to eat a snack. We arrived at the junction just as Peter pulled up. He'd been looking all over for us. There seems to have been a bit of confusion as to which route we were taking.

We stop and wait for Cynthia and Tilly to get out of the van to walk the last 500 yards with us. People in the hotel at the road junction notice our bucket and give us encouraging waves. Peter and Hazel pass us as we dawdle down the road. "Where's the finishing line?" we yell as we approach the car park.

"There isn't one," they reply. "There's one somewhere, I've seen a photograph of it in George Jones' book," Kathy yelled back. We finally see a sign that says 'End to Enders this way' and find the finishing line. Peter disappears to get his camera. Cynthia follows him. Ken follows them to get our official form from the van. Kathy just stands there. Hazel has her camera ready so Kathy takes our camera out of her pocket to give to Hazel and inadvertently crosses the finishing line on her own. "Get back, you're two minutes early," yells Hazel.

Everyone returns with cameras and bits of paper and we finally cross the line, either one minute early or two minutes late, depending on who's watch you want to believe. It might seem a little silly, this business of crossing the finishing line at precisely 2.00pm on Sunday 3 December but various people had asked what time we planned to finish and the Lands End - John O'Groats organisation said in their information sheet "if you don't let us know when you are arriving we can't arrange a welcome for you." Well, we did let them know.

The real reason for wanting to arrive when we said we would was about a sense of pride in the logistics. We had been at every one of our meeting points on time for the whole of the walk. Despite all that the weather had thrown at us in the south we had never been behind schedule and we just wanted the last step to be as precisely timed as the last 960 miles had been.

We're about to adjourn to the pub when a man by the official sign comes over to us and tells us he's been informed of our arrival and invites

us to be photographed, but not until we've paid for it. We feel a little bit miffed but he's only doing his job and they charge charity walkers half price so we cough up £3.50 and stand by his sign.

Next it's into the pub for the celebratory pint, write postcards to all the people who have given us a bed for the night and make four phone calls: one no reply, two answer phones and one to Mollie who was waiting to hear from us. The pub at John O'Groats is wonderful - two tellys

and slightly less customers if you don't count those five. There was a sign on the bar which read 'Please don't bore the barman' so we didn't. Tilly and me weren't allowed in of course. Not enough space.

'Mien host' finally asked us if we happened to be the Trimmers and manages to find a fax that Mollie had sent informing him of our arrival. There was not a word of welcome, neither from him or the Lands End - John O'Groats organisation. Hazel produced a card and a parcel containing a whole load of foot care stuff, which was very generous of her but completely unnecessary. The 2ks' feet are fine. The only time they had any problems was way down south.

They pile back into the van to drive the 80 miles back to Dornoch and we say farewell to Hazel as she sets off to pedal the fourteen miles back home. Like all our hosts, she had done us proud and we were delighted to have her support at the end.

A bath, and a drink with Cynthia, who has decided not to come out for dinner with us after all. At 84, she is allowed to have an early night when she wants one. The three of them walk down to the Castle Hotel for a lovely meal. The job is done.

First Day of the Real World - By Kathy
Monday, 4 December

We made a fond farewell to Cynthia, with a promise to visit her again soon   I didn't give John O'Groats a second glance yesterday; we never even saw the pier or walked to the edge. Today is different and as we approach the Dornoch Firth in the early morning light, tears stream down my face. The fellas are in the front and didn't see, thank goodness.

It seems immoral that we are going to drive back in one day a distance that has taken three weeks to walk. We cross the Cromarty Firth and stop to take a photograph, as it was too dark to photograph when we walked up. The seals were all asleep still. We're soon over Kessock Bridge and we can see the entrance to the Caladonian Canal, which we hadn't seen on the way up because we'd been on the other side of the road. Next it's Shochd Summit and the Dromacter Pass and we have a lovely view across Loch Garry.

Then it starts to rain. Apart from the last hour to Dalwhinney more than a week ago, it's the first rain we've seen since we've been in Scotland. By the time we got to Pitlochry it was pouring down and adding a pathetic finish to the Christmas decoration in the main street. My thoughts turned back to Worcester, over a month ago when we first saw Christmas decorations, also in the rain. From then on we weren't really following our route.

PLANNING THE WALK

We wanted to avoid road walking and take in as many footpaths as possible. We took a road atlas, drew a line to the Bristol Channel and then consulted OS maps to find footpaths that would take us in a fairly straight line. From the Bristol Channel we mostly followed canals to Manchester and then to Hebden Bridge.

We walked part of the following canals:

Day 6	Grand Western Canal
Day 7	Taunton & Bridgewater Canal
Day 12-14	Stafford and Worcester Canal
Day 15	Trent & Mersey Canal
Day 16	Macclesfield Canal
Day 17	The High Peak Canal
Day 18	Rochdale Canal

We loosely followed the Pennine Way and the Craven Way to our 'home patch'. From then on, a lot of the planning was based on where we had friends in Scotland. We walked parts of the following long distance paths:

Day 1	Cornish Coastal Path
Day 3	Camel Way
Day 5	Talka Trail
Day 10	Severn Way
Day 17	The Middlewood Trail
Day 19 & 20	The Pennine Way
Day 21	The Craven Way
Day 22	The Dales Way
Day 23	The Coast to Coast Footpath
Day 26	The Cumbria Way
Day 29	Southern Uplands Way
Day 34-38	Glasgow to Inverness Cycle Track

AND THE AFTER THOUGHTS

The wind was at out backs for the whole journey and the sun shone almost every day. We were always one day behind or one day ahead of the floods in the south and in Scotland we walked in shirt-sleeves almost every day. We had serious rain for less than twenty of the 960 miles.

The generosity of the hospitality we received on our journey was incredible. We stayed with twenty different friends, we slept in our camper van for nine nights, our own bed for four nights and stayed at B&B's for three nights. We carried the bucket for the whole journey and almost every day someone put something into it. We raised £13,570 for the Rainbow Trust including donations from one or two people we gave sponsorship forms to on our way who didn't have any money on them at the time.

There were many highlights - finding ourselves in the wonderful Pennine landscape the day after leaving Manchester, being met by the clog dancers who danced out of Dent with us and walking with children from Orton and Ravenstonedale Schools.

The low times were few. The last mile sometimes seemed a long one but there was never a day when we weren't raring to go again. We were thankful to have the van and driver Peter Davies with us. His commitment and patience were invaluable and in return we treated him like Cinderella, jumping out of the van and leaving all our mess for him to clear up and we let him sleep in a tent at the side of the van whilst we wallowed in luxury on our spring interior mattress under our down duvet.

We were very sad that Ranger didn't do the whole walk, but with all the chaos with the floods it seemed more sensible for her to return home when the van went back. She joined us again for the middle bit when we were staying at Cold Keld and in Scotland when the van was with us again so she did about 500 miles.

We can't put into words how good it was - 43 days of pure escapism; getting up and not having to take any decisions on what to wear and what to do and being outside all day and every day in wonderful daylight at the darkest time of the year.

A very big THANK YOU to everyone who gave us beds, food, drinks and sponsorship.

More books from Hayloft

The Long Day Done by Jeremy Rowan-Robinson
(£9.50, ISBN 1 9045240 4 4)

Odd Corners in Appleby, Gareth Hayes
(£8.50, ISBN 1 9045240 0 1)

The Ghastlies, Trix Jones and Shane Surgey
(£3.99, ISBN 1 9045240 4 4)

The Maddison Lone, A Journalist's Journey Around Britain, Roy Maddison
(£11.00, 1 9045240 6 0)

Changing the Face of Carlisle, The Life and Times of Percy Dalton, City Engineer and Surveyor, 1926-1949, Marie K. Dickens
(£8, ISBN 0 9540711 9 0)

From Clogs and Wellies to Shiny Shoes, A Windermere Lad's Memories of South Lakeland, Miles R. M. Bolton
(£12.50, ISBN 1 9045240 2 8)

A History of Kaber, Helen McDonald and Christine Dowson,
(£8, ISBN 0 9540711 6 6)

The Gifkin Gofkins, Irene Brenan
(£2.50, ISBN 1 9045240 1 X)

A Dream Come True, the Life and Times of a Lake District National Park Ranger, David Birkett
(£5.50, ISBN 0 9540711 5 8)

Gone to Blazes, Life as a Cumbrian Fireman, David Stubbings
(£9.95, ISBN 0 9540711 4 X)

Changing Times, The Millennium Story of Bolton, Barbara Cotton
(£12.50, ISBN 0 9540711 3 1)

Better by Far a Cumberland Hussar, A History of the Westmorland and Cumberland Yeomanry, Colin Bardgett
(Hardback, £26.95, ISBN 0 9540711 2 3)
(Paperback, £16.95, ISBN 0 9540711 1 5)

Northern Warrior, the Story of Sir Andreas de Harcla, Adrian Rogan
(£8.95, ISBN 0 9523282 8 3)

A Riot of Thorn & Leaf, Dulcie Matthews
(£7.95, ISBN 0 9540711 0 7)

A Country Doctor, Dr. Isaac Bainbridge, Dawn Robertson
(£2.25, ISBN 0 9523282 32)

Military Mountaineering, A History of Services Expeditions, 1945-2000,
Retd. SAS Major Bronco Lane
(Hardback, £25.95, ISBN 0 9523282 1 6)
(Paperback, £17.95, ISBN 0 9523282 6 7)

2041 - The Voyage South, Robert Swan
(£8.95, 0 9523282 7 5)

Yows & Cows, A Bit of Westmorland Wit, Mike Sanderson
(£7.95, ISBN 0 9523282 0 8)

Riding the Stang, Dawn Robertson
(£9.99, ISBN 0 9523282 2 4)

Secrets and Legends of Old Westmorland,
Peter Koronka and Dawn Robertson
(Hardback, £17.95, ISBN 0 9523282 4 0)
(Paperback, £11.95, ISBN 0 9523282 9 1)

The Irish Influence, Migrant Workers in Northern England,
Harold Slight
(£4.95, 0 9523282 5 9)

Soldiers and Sherpas, A Taste for Adventure, Brummie Stokes.
(£19.95, 0 9541551 0 6)

North Country Tapestry, Sylvia Mary McCosh
(£10, 0 9518690 0 0)

Between Two Gardens, The Diary of two Border Gardens,
Sylvia Mary McCosh
(£5.95, 0 9008111 7 X)

Dacre Castle, A short history of the Castle and the Dacre Family,
E. H. A. Stretton
(£5.50, 0 9518690 1 9)

*Antarctica Unveiled, Scott's First Expedition and the Quest for the
Unknown Continent,* David E. Yelverton
(£25.99, 0 8708158 2 2)

You can order any of our books by writing to:
Hayloft Publishing,
South Stainmore, Kirkby Stephen,
Cumbria, CA17 4EU, UK.
Please enclose a cheque plus £2 for UK postage and packing.
or telephone: +44 (0)17683) 42300
For more information see: www.hayloft.org.uk